VOYAGES

VOYAGES

AT SEA WITH STRANGERS

JOAN SKOGAN

A Saturday Night Book

HarperCollins*PublishersLtd*

The names of some people and some ships have been changed.

"The Redemption of Nick Carriere" appeared in *West Coast Review*; "Radio Silence" in *Grain*; "Every Summer Up the Coast" and "On *Provideniia*" in *Saturday Night*. A version of "At Sea with Strangers" (entitled "Eighty Plus One: A Woman At Sea") was broadcast on CBC and in Polish on Polskie Radio, Warsaw; "After the War" (entitled "Remembrance Day") and portions of "On *Provideniia*" were broadcast on CBC.

Permissions appear on page 149.

First Edition

Canadian Cataloguing in Publication Data

Skogan, Joan, 1945-
  Voyages: at sea with strangers

"A Saturday night book"
ISBN: 0-00-223756-6

1. Skogan, Joan, 1945- . 2. Seafaring life -
Canada. 3. Fishery law and legislation - Canada.
4. Canada. Dept of Fisheries and Oceans -
Biography. I. Title.

SH223.S56A3 1992   354.710082'362'092 C92-093491-9

92 93 94 95 96 ❖ RRD 5 4 3 2 1

I am grateful for the skill and generosity of the fisher-men I worked with, and for the patient efforts of Dianna Symonds, who edited the book and encouraged me, and Dianne de Gayardon de Fenoyl and Elizabeth Schaal, who checked the manuscript. Any errors are my own.

The crew may leave a ship. Their stories never leave. A story penetrates the whole ship and every part of it, the iron, the steel, the wood, all the holds, the coal-bunkers, the engine-hall, the stoke hold, even the bilge. Out of these parts, full of hundreds and thousands of stories, tales, and yarns, the ship tells the stories over again, with all the details and minor twists. She tells the stories to her best comrades – that is, to the members of the crew. She tells the stories better and more exactly than they could ever be told in print. One has only to listen with an understanding heart and with love for the ship.

—B. Traven
The Death Ship

THE REDEMPTION OF NICK CARRIERE

I think about Nick Carriere almost every night now when I can't sleep. First I think about my husband and how I left him and found another man and then left him. I go over the lying I've done to get money. Lie is too strong a word, I tell myself. I mean exaggerating the truth, fudging and softening and blurring it on government forms and applications for jobs and loans. Then I switch to thinking about Nick. The way he told it, he's walking in the Garden of Eden right here on earth now, after years in the wilderness, but his happy ending doesn't comfort me the way I always think it will.

The ferry was getting out into Milbanke Sound and Nick and Tommy Jack and I were the only ones left in the bar. This was last March, after herring.

"It was a dark and stormy night," Nick said solemnly, then he laughed and pulled back the heavy curtain so we could look out into the black and hear the crash of the sea. Tommy grinned. I used to know his father years ago in Alert Bay and they look alike. Nick was a stranger to me but he seemed peaceful enough. His eyes were light grey, like mine.

We were all quiet for a while, holding on to our glasses and watching the floor tilt back and forth. "You were fishing at Kitkatla?" I asked. Tommy nodded and he and Nick talked about the boats that had been there and the pools they were in and how much their own shares might be. Maybe I looked as if I were listening, but I wasn't. I was thinking about the last time I had crossed Milbanke Sound, getting a free ride south along with the chum salmon on a pig of a steel packer with a skipper to match. I walked off in Namu and demanded a different boat. I had been able to afford a high horse when I was still married to a good fisherman. I hitched my chair into the circle of light around the table and wondered if any other boats were travelling in the heaving darkness outside the curtained window.

Nick and Tommy were silent again. After a bit, I said, "Prices not bad, eh?" and Tommy told me the gillnet and seine prices for a ton of herring. I tried to look calm, as if I were expecting to help spend someone's crew share cheque, same as usual. Nick looked past Tommy and me onto the polished square of the empty dance floor.

"I had to fish for the Royal Bank once," he said. Tommy and I waited. I can't say if I knew it would be a funny story or a sad one, though Nick's mouth was already set in a hard line. I don't think even Nick knew, at the start, that he was going to line up his last thirty years and mark them off with stories like signposts on the road to where he lives now.

"Fishing for the Royal Bank," Nick repeated. "This was maybe thirty years ago, the branch at Main and Hastings. Fishermen are always saying they're fishing for the bank, eh. Paying off their boat loans. But this bank was actually giving the orders. They had a hold on Eddie and John Johansen for the *Katherine A.* and they wouldn't take the boat back − no market − and they wouldn't let go. It was, 'Take the boat out again. Find fish. Make money.'" Maybe Tommy was listening because there was nothing else to listen to. He might not have had that much experience with banks. But I was paying close attention. I like a good bank story.

Nick went on. "This was in November. Eddie and John − Johnny's dead now − they'd gone broke buying salmon in the Charlottes and I'd been on the boat with them since May. I'd never have got any of my share if I quit them then. No other jobs around anyway. Only thing we had gear for that was around that time of year was dogfish." Nick sighed. Tommy and I looked sympathetic. A story with dogfish and the Royal Bank and November in it was not going to end well.

Nick passed lightly over six weeks' longlining in the Straits. Wind. Rain. Cold. More potatoes than anything else to eat. Some dogfish. Eight cents a pound, dressed. The *Katherine A.* didn't make grub and fuel. "Two days before Christmas we dumped the last load at Campbell Avenue. Walked up to the bank. They had a young fellow in there, real snotty, with a nice suit."

Nick's voice stayed quiet but he spat out his words like birdshot. "'We need a drag,' Eddie says to this young banker. 'A drag,' the banker says back. 'What's a drag?'" Nick stopped for a moment so we could take this in. I thought about it. The Royal Bank had apparently thought that being a fishing company meant sending its boat out to work but having nothing to do with the men who had to kneel on her deck and fillet dogfish in the rain.

"Finally," said Nick, "the little banker caught on. 'You can have twenty-five dollars,' he said. Eddie and John didn't say nothing, just stared at the floor. Too beat down, I guess. But I grabbed the little prick and lifted him off his feet. 'That's not enough for a hooker and a steak,' I yelled, 'and how are we supposed to get home for Christmas?'"

Tommy chuckled softly and Nick smiled but his mouth returned right away to its tight line. I wondered what was coming next. I figured the big money on this year's herring had put Nick in mind of harder times and he didn't look, right then, as if he was finished remembering them.

Tommy went up to the bar to get us more drinks and I watched him coming back, walking easily, even with the floor slanting and dropping under him, and lifting the three glasses a little at the bottom of the roll so they wouldn't spill when the ship rose again. He sat down and Nick said, "My son was born not too long after." The baby was fine at first, Nick told us, then something went wrong. He took a year to die. This was before the medical plan, so the bills were high.

Nick got the money robbing banks. The Kingsway and Knight branch of the Bank of Montreal and the one on Columbia Street in New Westminster; the Bank of Nova Scotia at Main and 2nd; the Toronto Dominion out in Abbotsford and the Bank of Commerce in Ladner, plus four or five more. "No Royal Banks," Nick said. "Coincidence. Not in the right place at the right time." Doing banks was not that tough, Nick assured us.

"Did you get caught?" I asked. Nick laughed.

"Do enough banks and for sure you'll get caught," he answered. Tommy looked thoughtful and I tried to look as though I knew that all along. As for Nick, remembering prison didn't seem to bother him. Maybe he looked on jail as a natural consequence of bank robbing, just something to be postponed as long as possible.

The ferry heeled hard and Tommy reached out to save the ashtray. I got up and went to the bar to get a coffee. Nick and Tommy didn't want anything. When I got back to the table, they were both laughing. I didn't ask why.

Nick was in jail a long time. When he got out, he hooked up with a friend who had a log salvage licence. "You know how they work?" Nick asked me. "Used to work, anyway. A log salvage licence and a chain saw and you're in business. A licence to steal. We were putting together a boom, see. Courtesy of Mac. and Blo. and Rayonier. Get thirty-five, maybe forty thousand for it. We just needed someone to back us for the tug and the fuel. So I got five thousand from a guy I knew in Vancouver. Guaranteed him it would triple in a month."

Six weeks later the boom lay in a bay south of Powell River and Nick and his partner and the man from Vancouver were sitting on the bed in a room in the Austin Hotel on Granville Street. "Had the money," Nick said. "No problem. Thirty-seven thousand. Fifteen for the guy who backed us. Eleven each for my partner and me. I'm just counting out the fifteen when the door flies open. In comes a guy carrying a chunk. Points it at the guy who backed us. Says, 'He owes me.' Who's going to argue? I made a move to hand over the stack, twelve thousand and some. 'No,' says the guy with the gun. 'Take him over by the window.' So we do. Guy says, 'He goes out and you two get your share. If I have to do it, you get nothing.'"

Nick looked into my eyes for the first time. "What would you do?" he said to me. I stared back at him. I knew, even then, that he wanted me to say there was common ground between us. He knew what I would have done. I'm certain he knew. The backer was gone whatever Nick, or I, would have decided to do. I didn't answer and he didn't ask again.

Nick said in a low voice that he had hit the backer very hard on the side of the neck, then he and his partner opened the window on the fourth floor of the Austin Hotel and shoved him out.

Nick got up and went to the washroom and was gone for a long time. Tommy drew his chair closer to mine and searched his shirt pocket. He took out a handful of wooden matches and arranged them on the table to make fish shapes with squared-off fins. "There," he murmured, "sockeye swimming north. See if you can move four matches and make them swim south." I stared at the matchstick fish for a long time before I reached out to move one match. My hand shook. "That's right," Tommy said encouragingly, "that's a start." Then he said, very quietly, "Nicky's a good man on the boat. He's all right. Don't say anything too hard to him." I nodded my head.

Nick sat down with us again. It was after midnight by then and the swell had gone down. We were almost across the Sound. Nick was watching me and I sat very still. He spoke slowly. "I was in Lillooet a while afterwards. Never been there before or since. I was helping my uncle move some stuff. We went into the Legion." My back was beginning to ache from being held so stiffly. "There was a woman in the Legion," Nick said. "Japanese. Shy. Always lived in Lillooet, never been in the Legion before in her life."

Nick pulled back the blackout curtain and held it so I could see over his shoulder. Outside was as black as ever, but the sound of the waves had fallen. When he turned back from the window, his face looked smoother, younger. "I thought it was all over when I got back to Vancouver, and the cops picked me up for some court show I missed. My uncle told her about it. She sent down the bail money."

Tommy seemed relaxed, not surprised. I suppose I wasn't that startled, either. From the start of the Lillooet story, Nick had looked happier, his mouth in a gentle curve. Nick and the Japanese woman live in Nanoose, in a house hidden off the road. Nick has worked on the same seine boat for herring and salmon more than ten years now, and he makes good money. He tells the fishing company to send his cheques straight home. Nick said the woman has been cautious and clever with the money. They own another place as well as their own house and are quite secure, the two of them.

When I can't sleep, I prop all four pillows behind my head so I'm half sitting up in the dark. After I'm done remembering my husband and the other man and lies about money, I start on Nick Carriere's stories, certain that I'll be able to rest if I can come to understand why Nick got lucky or received the grace of God or whatever it was that provided the Japanese woman. She saved him, after all. Redeemed him.

I get up and fill the kettle for tea on particularly long nights. While I wait for the water to boil, I stand by the bookcase in the hall, running my fingers along the top row of books, looking, perhaps, as if I might choose any one of them. Then I pull out the dictionary and check once more. "Redeem: To recover by expenditure of effort or buy back one's rights, position, honour, or pledged goods. To purchase the freedom of another or oneself. *Of God or Christ*: To deliver from sin or damnation. To make amends for, counterbalance, or compensate." The dictionary says nothing of how to earn redemption.

When I drink my tea and finish with the night on the ferry last March, when I have remembered everything about Milbanke Sound and Nick's face and Tommy's matchstick fish, it is that unearned, accidental quality about Nick's happiness that denies me the comfort of believing it could happen to me. Nick did nothing to deserve the Japanese woman. He told the truth. I give him that.

I smooth the sheets and lie down again and pretend the bed is rocking on a gentle swell. I open my eyes to see if the sky is lighter yet and wonder if I would still be married if I'd known how this would be. I listen for the sound of the waves on my imagined sea, but most nights I can hear only the hard grinding of the stones on the bottom.

I was in Lillooet last May. I stopped at the Legion but there was nothing there for me, and I drove through to the coast that same night.

EVERY SUMMER
UP THE COAST

Jackie Bass drowned on the halibut last year. I remember exactly where I was when the news came on the
radio. I was driving back and forth between Spanish
Banks and the lookout, pretending the Skeena River
was going to appear around every curve in the road. I
was concentrating so hard I missed the names of the
men the Coast Guard helicopter picked up off the deck
of their boat, which was sliding into the sea outside of
Masset Inlet. I turned up the radio and heard about the
two bodies found farther south, still floating in their
survival suits. Then Jackie in Hecate Strait. I was
close to the lookout by then, so I stopped there and
stared at the log booms lining the shore along the
river mouth.

I knew Jackie the whole time I was in Prince Rupert. He was one of the boys from Lesser Slave Lake who caught on to fishing the coast so fast. The fishing companies started going out to Alberta to get those Cree fishermen when they missed the Japanese during the war. Not that Jackie was anything like that old. He was around my age, dark-haired and quick, smiled a lot and did fine gillnetting most seasons.

I saw him in early summer every year in the little bar that used to be out at Port Edward on the Skeena slough. We'd have a reunion. Was I working? Was Jackie's boat okay? No disasters for either of us over the winter? Questions done, we could grin at each other and drink beer and talk about the night we met.

I met Jackie in the Prince Rupert Hotel the first summer I was up north. I still had my work boots on, but I took them off and we danced until the bar closed, then we drove out to Kloiya Creek in someone's truck. This was before I knew anyone else up there. The years afterwards, we would have this little time together in the bar at Port Edward before salmon started, then Jackie would go back to his nets and I would go back to town.

At the lookout, I pictured Jackie's body in the grey, tilting sea. I was better satisfied with this new sorrow than with my own longing for the north coast. I didn't shed any tears, but I sat in my car staring at the Fraser long enough to call it mourning.

When I saw Jackie on the Steveston dock this summer I put my arms around him so he couldn't drift beyond my reach again. I thought you were dead, I told him.

Everyone heard he had drowned, Jackie said, because he leased out his halibut licence and the radio got the wrong name when the boat went down. We sat on the edge of the dock and asked each other the usual questions, then there was a silence between us. Jackie wanted to go up to the hotel for a beer. I said I would meet him there, but I drove back to the city instead, trying to figure out all the way across the bridge how and where and why, let alone of what, Jackie had cheated me.

ON *PROVIDENIIA*

"... he said, 'I know of a cure for everything: salt water.'
'Salt water?' I asked him.
'Yes,' he said, 'in one way or the other. Sweat, or tears, or the salt sea.'"

—Isak Dinesen
Seven Gothic Tales

She sits beside the fishery officer in the captain's cabin, wearing her boarding-a-new-ship clothes. First and most important, three-year-old black high-top runners, faded and frayed from salt water, laced with net twine. The trawl bo's'n on her last ship the year before took them apart, scraped, glued, and clamped them so they would last one more season. The Polish fishermen know she can't judge the instant the rising swell peaks, then jump from the lifeboat to the rope ladder without her magic shoes. Forget the Poles, she tells herself and feels her mouth tremble. She covers her lips with her hand and pretends to study the portrait of Lenin hanging over the captain's desk.

The fishery officer beside her sips vodka and recites the latitude and longitude for the boundaries of offshore fishing areas 5-1a, 5-1b, and 5-2 to *Provideniia*'s third officer, who is translating for the captain. She estimates the third officer is getting about one-quarter of what the fishery officer says and giving the captain less than that. She knows she will live with these gaps for the next ninety days and decides not to take off her sunglasses yet.

She looks down. The shoes, at least, have not failed her. She is, by the grace of God and the black runners, on board, up the ladder one more time. She congratulates herself for not wearing too-tight jeans, slides a finger under her belt. Leather. Western. Thrift shop, Albuquerque, New Mexico, 1978. Now too snug. She will lose weight starting tomorrow, climbing from the factory below decks up to the bridge, running to the stern every time *Provideniia* hauls fish, lifting fish baskets, being awake eighteen hours a day.

She slips her pearls outside the collar of her jean jacket and spreads a careful, close-mouthed smile around the captain's cabin for the benefit of the man from Immigration and the customs officer, a woman wearing far too much make-up, along with the tall, bulky Russian sitting with them at the captain's table.

She includes the captain in the smile. He is too young, she has decided. The big man must be the commissar. Problems ahead. Get off the ship, she silently orders the customs woman, the man from Immigration, and the fishery officer. You have no idea what it's like alone out here with them. Get off and let me get on with it.

She clears her throat and speaks for the first time on *Provideniia*. "Please tell the captain there is no dumping in Canadian waters," she says to the fishery officer.

"I'm sure he ..."

Her voice comes out thin and cold. "Please tell him." The third officer translates. The captain nods.

She hears briefcases being snapped shut. She remembers now how she lulls herself into believing that whatever is happening at sea will go on forever. When there is only a broad, low swell offshore, the sea will lie calm under a clear sky always. When it blows and the ship and the sea slam together, the world will never be quiet again. When there are a hundred tons of hake a day, there will always be fish. Now, she is astonished at how quickly Customs and Immigration and Fisheries are gone. Feels a flicker of malicious pleasure when the made-up customs woman stumbles turning to grip the stanchions at the top of the ladder and has to be grabbed by a small gypsy who must be the deck bo's'n. The ladder is hauled. The tug moves away. She waves and turns from the deck rail.

The gypsy has disappeared, along with the captain. She is alone on the boat deck. She can't remember where her cabin is and her cheeks warm with shame and awkwardness when she looks up to the storm bridge and sees a dark-haired man, probably the chief mate, watching her.

Would you rather have had a man to work with you? she wants to ask him. I know you'd rather not have a fishery observer at all, of course. Maybe a younger woman? a thinner one? with longer hair and bigger breasts? one who smiles more, who won't stand at the bridge window when she is exhausted, staring at the sea in the dark? one who doesn't smoke as much as you do yourself?

You don't understand, she would like to call up to him. I'm not like the others they've told you about. I never complain about the cockroaches and the food. I know my job. There won't be any trouble. You'll see.

The dark-haired man lifts a microphone. His order is blown away on the wind, but she hears the anchor chains clanging on the bow. *Provideniia* shudders slightly and slowly begins to make way, turning north up Juan de Fuca Strait and picking up speed.

There is a pane of glass between the Russians and me when I first board *Provideniia*. We can see each other and sometimes make out gestures or a few words through this glass wall, but nothing more.

The ship is fishing hake off the west coast of Vancouver Island and we can sometimes see Amphitrite Point light at the mouth of Barkley Sound off the bow, but we are in another, harder country. The faces of the officers and crew are often turned away from me.

Provideniia, 2800 gross tons, home port Petropavlovsk, U.S.S.R., is one of six Soviet ships licensed to take Canada's unused hake stocks in our waters. Her captain and crew members won't get beyond the Bering Sea again unless they fulfil the production quotas given to them by Soviet authorities. They must also comply with Canadian fishing regulations or risk being sent back to Petropavlovsk. Their licence requires them to carry a Canadian fishery observer to record their catch and monitor all of their fish-processing operations.

When I begin work as the fishery observer on *Provideniia*, I become the "foreign woman." No-one is permitted to be alone with me. Doors must be left open if I am present. In the factory below decks, the workers press their bodies into the edge of the fish lines and never look up from the heading and gutting machines when I pass behind them. The men I meet in the passageways stand back against the bulkhead, holding themselves stiffly, turning their heads away, until I walk by. On *Provideniia*, the openness of *glasnost* and the new thinking of *perestroika* do not touch us any more than we touch each other.

I am tempted hourly to abandon the Russians, to stop trying to soften their hard faces and convince them to trust me. I am tempted to hide from them behind a hardness of my own.

Provideniia is a stern trawler. She catches fish by towing a bag-shaped net called a codend fastened to half a kilometre or more of trawl wire through the sea behind her. On joint venture, the smaller Canadian trawlers sell their catch to the foreign ships. The Canadian boats fishing for *Provideniia* fasten their full codends to the hawser line trailing in our wake. The codend, *kutok* in Russian, crammed with as much as twenty-five tons of hake, is hauled back to the stern ramp by the main winch, shackled to a block, and pulled up the ramp onto the trawl deck. The tons of hake are dumped into tanks feeding onto the fish lines in the factory below decks.

Each day for the first few weeks' fishing on *Provideniia*, the same problems occur again and again.

No-one lets me know we are hauling, although they know I must be on deck to look at every codend. *Provideniia* hauls six or seven times a day if we are getting at least ten tons in each codend, more often if we are not. I hear the winches screaming and run down to the trawl deck, then shuffle across its tilting surface, weaving and staggering beside the strung-tight lines, because no-one said we were hauling so I could get to the stern safely before we start. On the bridge, they thought someone in the factory would tell me. In the factory, they thought the trawl crew would let me know.

Reasonable deck estimates of *Provideniia*'s catch are required. The factory manager will say fourteen metric tons of hake for every codend whether the net is crammed with twenty tons or sagging with only eight. Beside the factory manager on the storm bridge above the trawl deck, the captain stands smiling with his hands behind his back. Deck estimation is not his job.

The ship's deck estimate must include the by-catch, anything other than hake. *Provideniia*'s fishing logs will list 400 kilograms of dogfish for a haul that contained at least two tons of these fish mixed in with the hake. When the next codend does hold only 400 kilograms of dogfish, the deck estimate shows a ton. Going down on deck to look at the codend or checking the tanks in the factory is not the factory manager's job.

All by-catch must be set aside for the observer to see. No lingcod, no yellowtail rockfish, no red snapper appear in *Provideniia*'s deck estimates or in the factory, although I see them in the codend. The factory foreman points downwards. We both stare at the line running past our boots, carrying guts and fish too crushed to process down to the fish-meal plant. Neither the captain nor the factory manager told the foreman and his workers to set aside the cod and other fish for me to look at.

My knees lock sometimes during the circuit from my cabin down to the factory, up to the trawl deck, up again to the captain's cabin and the bridge, back down to the factory. My hands shake and the soup quivers in my spoon when I sit across from the commissar in the officers' mess. I lift my eyes only to glance at the two men watching us from their portraits on the bulkheads. Lenin looks disdainful. He expected better production from *Provideniia*. Mikhail Gorbachev is mild and thoughtful. He is waiting, perhaps, to see what we will do with the rest of the hake season.

I carry the Oxford Russian dictionary in my hip pocket along with the fishing regulations translated into

Russian. Every day, I explain the solutions to the problems again: the deck estimates, the fishing logs, the necessary accounting for any fish we catch other than hake. There is no punishment for this by-catch, I say. We must just tell the truth about it. *Pravda*. Only *pravda*. After a while, I yell. One day, I pound my fist.

When I walk into the factory in the evening of the fist-pounding day, everything is as it was early in the morning, as it was before dinner and after dinner, in the mid- and late afternoon, as it always is in the factory. The tanks pour streams of hake onto the lines. The floor grating is still broken in four places and water slides back and forth beneath it as the ship rolls. The grinding screech of the gutting machines rises and falls, punctuated by the slam of frozen hake blocks being jarred from their trays. The smell of fish is strong, and, in the crowded spaces behind the tanks, sour. Four portholes are grimed with salt and scales. Two are open on round-framed pictures of a perfectly proportioned world, one-third bluish-grey sea, two-thirds darkening sky. A blurred band of red marks the meeting place between sky and sea.

I move sideways beside the fish line, squeezing myself behind the row of blue-shirted backs. Near the chute where hake are falling from the tanks onto the line, there is something new. A pile of fish has been laid on the grating, heads to the bow, tails to the stern. Fourteen widow rockfish, and lying beside the stubby-bodied widows, a lingcod. By-catch set aside for the observer.

Every man on the line is bent over his machine. Every face is hidden. Across the factory, Yuri, the foreman, turns to avoid my glance and looks intently into the viewing port on the tank beside him.

I want to laugh until I cry. I want to smile at every man down here and have them smile back. I want to shake Yuri's hand. Instead, I put an expression of grave satisfaction on my face and edge past the *tushka* machine so I can go up to the trawl deck and get the fish scales and basket to weigh the cod.

Every day I work in the captain's cabin on *Provideniia*'s paper problems, beginning in the middle of the morning. I sit at his table facing the starboard side windows with the national fishing log, the joint-venture log, my notebooks, and my calculator spread before me. The captain smiles gently, pleased that I am here to keep him company, and resumes reading his novel. On *Provideniia*, the captain and the commissar do not work a minimum twelve hours a day as the rest of the crew does.

Every log entry for the previous day's catch before midnight must be checked. Trawl number, time, latitude and longitude, average trawl depth are all compared with the figures in my notebook. Yesterday's deck estimates for the tons of fish in each haul are now only a matter for regret and hope for better things today.

I straighten my back and sigh when I begin on the factory production figures. They must be calculated with a conversion rate, a decimal fraction that reflects the efficiency of the machinery converting whole fish to a frozen product.

16.56 metric tons of frozen headed and gutted times 1.785 equals 29.56 tons of whole fish. Plus the *tushka* equals 48.09 tons caught yesterday. The ship's total estimate is 51 tons of hake. Mine is just over 47 tons. Fine. Reasonable differences except that neither 47 nor 48 nor 51 tons is enough fish to satisfy *Provideniia*'s production quota.

Every four or five days, the captain demonstrates his concern over our production. The demonstration begins with the captain staring out the starboard windows at the horizon until I notice he is doing so. I put down my pencil and wait. If the catch has averaged less than fifty tons for some days, he may call the third officer to translate. Otherwise, he makes do with the dictionary and my sympathy. Mention is made of small sons and daughters back in Leningrad, of the onerous and difficult-to-comprehend Canadian regulations. Responsibility for the poor catch is assigned to the chief mate, to the Canadian trawlers, to life. *Taková zhizn'*. That's life. By this time, I am staring out the window at the horizon too. We both sigh. The captain picks up his book. I begin to write and calculate again. I have reached the fish-meal production figures in the logs.

The meal plant is far below. One deck beneath the captain's cabin, where the only signs of hake are the scales that drift from my hair to settle on the cloth-covered table, is the trawl deck. Below the trawl deck is the factory and behind the tanks in the factory are the narrow stairs leading down to the fish-meal plant. Most people on *Provideniia*, including the captain, never go to the meal plant. Tons of guts and unwanted fish are piped down here, boiled, chopped, dried, and ground into flaked meal for fertilizer or animal feed. The two men who work in the plant are paid a bonus. The fish-meal plant is a version of hell without the open flames, but I don't mind it.

The roar of the machinery makes speech or hearing impossible, so if I want to know anything about the operation, I have to climb up the catwalk and look for myself, or beckon the workers to come back to the meal hold.

In the meal hold, the sour stink of old fish becomes lighter, drier, and there are signs of land – rats; wood, which lines the cargo bulkheads; and a smell like grain, from the burlap meal sacks. On *Provideniia*, there are two shades of brown sacks and one striped pattern. The meal-hold man gives me one of each. Because of these bags jammed under my arm, I hear a whispered greeting in the factory for the first time. "*Da, da*," I turn around and whisper back, "Robin Hood."

The meal sacks hold forty-five kilograms, so, sweating by now in the captain's too-warm cabin, I multiply forty-five times however many bags to get the tonnage of fish meal made yesterday. This number along with the figures for fresh fish, frozen products, tonnage of guts, and the theoretical meal-plant conversion rate whirl through my calculator and around again in a back calculation. Every morning my figures show we have either too much meal – the factory manager's conversion rate is wrong – or too little – some of the guts must have been dumped overboard, against the fishery regulations, or the product numbers in the logs are wrong.

Every morning, I get up from the table and carry the logs to the captain's desk to show him the imbalance. I sit down again while he telephones the factory manager to demand his presence. The captain plugs in his kettle to make coffee and we wait. The kettle will take five minutes to come to a full boil, and by that time the factory manager will be here. He will take between ten and thirty minutes to decide that it is true there is some mistake in the logs. The captain will ask if I really do not want any sugar in my coffee. The factory manager will say this mistake will never happen again. The three of us will nod gravely to one another, finish our coffee, and go our separate ways until tomorrow morning.

On some mornings in the captain's cabin, the pattern between the two of us is disrupted. Perhaps yesterday's catch was especially poor and the captain will be reading from the *Collected Works* of Lenin and will not look up when I enter. Perhaps the paper problems will be more dramatic than usual and I will be angry instead of wearily matter-of-fact. The captain will say he is sending the factory manager back to Petropavlovsk on the mother ship. I will say I think this problem will diminish and surely we do not need to be so harsh.

I learn quickly not to present the captain with much more than minor discrepancies. To solve problems, he has the commissar and a black book for listing crew members' fines or other punishments to take place during or after this voyage. It is necessary some mornings in the captain's cabin for me to call him "Captain Gorbachev" – and deflect his attention from some crew member or officer he has decided to blame for everything that is wrong on *Provideniia*.

Most mornings, we are peaceful enough, the captain and I.

At night on *Provideniia*, I work in my cabin between 2200 and midnight. I sit at the plywood table bolted to the bulkhead and switch on the small light that encloses only my body, the chair, and the table, leaving the bunk and the pile of duffel bags behind me in darkness. Over my left shoulder, the open porthole lets the sound of the sea rushing past our hull into the cabin.

I dig two spoonfuls of Soviet instant coffee out of the tin under the table and dump them into an enamel cup, then reach down for the pickle jar filled with fresh water. The 220-volt immersion heater Alyosha gave me bubbles the coffee in less than a minute.

While I work on diagrams of *Provideniia*'s factory and fish-meal plant, I hear Morse code and static from the radio room across the passageway. Prokofiev floats up from the lower deck where the intercom is broadcasting Moscow Radio. Sometimes I hear footsteps and low voices when Viktor, the deck bo's'n, and his crew pass by my porthole on the boat deck. They are prohibited from stopping outside my cabin.

As I look up from my papers, I see Anna Akhmatova's poem taped to the bulkhead beside the light. An

S-shaped hook made from rusted wire dangles in front of her words:

> To earthly solace, heart be not a prey
> To wife and home do not attach yourself,
> Take the bread out of your child's mouth,
> And to a stranger give the bread away.
> Become the humblest servant to the man
> Who was your blackest enemy,
> Call by your brother's name the forest wolf,
> And do not ask God for anything.

On the shelf above the poem are the books left in my cabin by the commissar: *Prisoners of Conscience in the U.S.S.R. and Their Patrons; The Soviet Army and the People; Peace is the Chief Thing; The U.S.S.R. Yearbook; The October Revolution and Perestroika; Soviet Cinema; Problems of Adolescents in the Soviet Union; Stories of the Revolution for Young People.*

From this last book, I have memorized four lines from a revolutionary song. Now, some nights when I am checking *Provideniia*'s fishing logs again and again with my own weekly totals, I mutter to myself, "How many on our flesh have fattened/ But if these bloody birds of prey/ Shall vanish from the sky one morning/ The golden sunlight still will stay."

As *Provideniia* moves through the night, I will continue to draw lines, label machine diagrams, and enter computer codes on biological data forms, leaning out of the light now and then to look out the porthole into the dark. I will make another cup of coffee and watch for a moment as its surface divides into concentric, trembling rings, shaken by the rhythm of the main engines three decks below. I will light a Russian cigarette, the kind we call diesel brand, and work at the table in my cabin until something changes on *Provideniia*. The wind picks up or dies down. *Provideniia* increases speed or changes course or begins to drift. The helmsman comes to tell me we are going to make a last, late haul. Yuri, the foreman in the factory, sends up a message about dogfish mixed in with the hake. At midnight, the crew in the factory will have a tea break and I might go down and do a conversion test on the heading machines with them when they return to work.

I will stand and stretch, pick up my knife, which lies on top of Mikhail Sergeyevich's dictionary. In this dictionary, published in Moscow in 1973, are words for: playfellow, sensation-monger, birchen (which is right after birch), and many birds – of feather, of passage, and queer birds. There are also words for antitank and daughter missile.

I will put on my jacket and boots, kick the life belt back under the bunk, not let myself look at the sheets buttoned over wool blankets and the huge feather pillow on top of the bunk. If I look in the small mirror beside the door, I will see a physical resemblance between my son and me for the first time in my life. When he was small, his face often carried the same expression of polite interest tempered with caution that my face shows now. Most nights, there will be a smear of fish blood on my cheek. I will scrub it off and step into the passageway beyond my cabin, leaving the small light burning until I return.

The linoleum on the floor of *Provideniia*'s main-deck passageway has been trodden into a ragged brown track bordered with blue. My boots clump wide of this path as I pitch from side to side, until I give in and use the handrail on the stairs. The roll is slower below decks, but down here when we run fast at nights, I think I hear someone whispering my name, "Zhona, Zhona," the way the Russians say it, under the rumble of the main engines. But all of the cabin doors are closed. It is forbidden for the crew to stand in the passageways.

Tonight, even the factory at the stern end of this deck is empty and silent. There will be no fish on board, no deck estimates of hake and yellowtail rockfish or factory production numbers to argue about, no fist pounding, no problems until tomorrow. We have to steam another sixty miles from the mother ship until we reach the fishing grounds again. Except for the second engineer and the motormen in the engine room beneath my feet, the radio officer dozing over his Moscow-time transmissions, and the helmsman and the chief mate on the bridge, *Provideniia* is sleeping.

The chief mate is a Mongol. His eyes and his thick, straight hair are dark brown. He has a gold tooth on the right side. He is exactly my height. He makes a small impatient sound in his throat when anyone talks too long on the bridge.

When the chief mate is on watch, he paces back and forth, leaning out the portside door for a few seconds, slamming it shut, then crossing to the windows over the bow and levering the centre window down, pushing it up a moment later. He crouches over the radar hood, muttering to himself, runs into the chart room to fix our position. He never looks up from his charts or his log entries until he is finished with them.

Now, four weeks into our voyage, the chief mate speaks to me sometimes. If Alexei, the helmsman, knocks at my door at 0530 and I go to the bridge with my dreams about the commissar making charlotte russe and my pearls losing their sheen still clustered around me, the chief mate will say, "Radio," and point to the VHF. When I mutter into the transmitter and hear only broken static back, he takes the handset and says firmly, "She want seven-two," and switches the channel. If it is blowing and I stumble into the radar, stringing the handset cord out to its limit and clutching at the starboard door fastening, he stands beside me and watches until I get my balance.

Night fishing, we stand together looking into the sounder screen at the orange and yellow dotted blurs showing schools of rockfish and herring, or bottom-feed, waiting for hake. When he opens the door to the deck, I look over his shoulder at the dark sea and the rain. He murmurs to himself in Russian and picks up the microphone to order the bo's'n to lower or raise our trawl wire. Only the sleeves of our identical, dark-green hooded coats touch. We pass the Russian-English dictionary back and forth, taking turns to look up words like searching, peak, snag, north, and difficult. One night, after three hours at the sounder screen, I look up the Russian word for magic.

"Magic" is one of the words the captain can't bear to hear. He doesn't like "soul" or "spirit" either, but I say these words now and then anyway during the hours I spend each day sitting at the table in his cabin poring over *Provideniia*'s logs. Sometimes I look them up, along with "courage" and "survival," to inspire the captain when there aren't enough fish.

Communication between the captain and me shattered for a week after I translated my occasional shivering in his overheated cabin into a bird flying over my grave. The captain will not even admit to dreaming, but gets up from his desk to make me another cup of coffee so I will stop talking about the "not reality."

The chief mate doesn't mind the notion of calling hake with magic though. He continues to look into the sounder screen and I lean on the ledge by the bow windows and look down into the sea, making myself believe I can see through layers of darkness to the drifting mass of fish thirty fathoms below. When we go back to the storm bridge together and the haul is twenty-five tons, we grin at each other like wolves. Then he gestures briskly towards the ladder and I run down to the trawl deck to watch the codend spilling into the tanks while he returns to the bridge.

But it is not until we off-load at *Chukotka*, the mother ship a hundred miles off Barkley Sound, that I know why Mikhail Sergeyevich, our trawl master, says the chief mate is a good man.

I am walking the dull brown track in the main-deck passageway again. For twenty-four fishing days, I have explained and checked and corrected the deck estimates and factory-production numbers recorded in *Provideniia*'s logs. Twenty-four mornings, I have watched the factory manager nod in agreement and listened to him, along with the captain, say it will be better tomorrow. Now, I cannot face the piles of paper and hours of calculation and fury needed to reconcile the difference between *Provideniia*'s logs and the tonnage we are transshipping to *Chukotka*.

I stop at the door to the chief mate's cabin. Usually his door is closed or his cabin is full of people wanting a different shift in the factory, but today he is alone, sitting at his typewriter, his face dark and serious. He looks up and nods and I step over the sill. I sit down across from him and he hands me the dictionary, but my anger over the factory manager's stubbornness is now awash with weariness and I can't decide which word to search for. "*Plokho*," I whisper at last. "*Plokho*." Bad. The chief mate looks at me carefully, then he gets up and closes his door.

The commissar's cabin is next to the chief mate's. Mikhail Sergeyevich says there are six informers on board. Only Katya from the kitchen or Irina, our doctor, ever sits next to me. It is forbidden for anyone from *Provideniia* to be alone with me. The chief mate gives no sign he is thinking about these things.

When I hear his door close, I remember that I have refused to weep on *Provideniia*. But when he sits down across from me again and says in careful, slow English, without the dictionary, "I think this work on our ship is hard for you," my tears gather and fall. He fumbles in the pocket of his coat hanging behind his chair and finds two cigarettes. We sit and smoke in silence and when my breathing evens out, he gets up and opens the door.

I go to my cabin and gather up the fishing logs. The chief mate is typing again when I stride past his door on my way to wake the factory manager and demand that he recalculate the meal-plant conversion rate.

Tonight, I pause at the top of the stairs on the upper deck, then turn towards the bridge and open the door. It is dark in here except for the tiny light by the tea stand on the port side. Alexei is at the wheel and after a moment, I see the chief mate bent over the radar beside him. The sky and the sea are a dark bulk around us, not a star or another ship in sight. Only our own running lights shine ahead. *Spokoinuyu noch'*, I say, and Alexei looks over his shoulder and nods. The chief mate doesn't look up from the radar, but his voice is quiet and familiar. "Good night, Zhona," he says. I close the bridge door and go to my cabin, take off my boots, lie down with my green coat over me, sink into the sway of the ship and sleep.

After more than forty days on *Provideniia*, I have forgotten the land. Days and nights blur together and when I lean on the stern deck rail, staring at the sea, waiting to haul, I seldom remember what I am thinking. Maybe, I am thinking how strange it is to live and work closely with so many people who know so little about me.

Anna is often with the commissar and the captain these days. I see her in the captain's cabin, her square body bent forward in her chair, her reddish-brown hair springing from its pins, her lips pressed tightly together as she listens to their lectures about poor work and loud laughter in the motormen's cabin some nights.

She is not permitted to say much in response and she looks angry. Anna is a great talker, a better talker than a cleaner, and cleaning is her job on *Provideniia*, along with her shift on the heading machine in the fish factory.

Anna is not a good cleaner. She sweeps the larger pieces of dirt in the passageways and the upper-deck cabins into piles with a twig broom, then wanders off to search unsuccessfully for a dustpan. When she returns, her heap of dust and hake scales is usually scattered. She shrugs and picks up what she can with her fingers. She never sweeps or mops under my bunk.

Anna does not have good timing. Often she knocks and flings open my door when I am lying down for the first time in eighteen hours and am supposed to be woken only if we are hauling. If I take five minutes off from my paperwork to read Marina Tsvetaeva, Anna is sure to want to pick up my laundry and babble at me in her mixture of Ukrainian and Russian while she minutely examines my camisoles and shirts and jeans. It is a sorrow to Anna that I must dress like a man, but she knows my underwear better than I do. Anna's curiosity is relentless.

The trawl deck is forbidden ground for her, but she peeks out from the main-deck passageway sometimes to watch me with the deck crew. She might see me slumped on the bench behind the main winch, propped up between Mikhail Sergeyevich, the trawl master, and Sasha, the youngest fisherman, who both disregard the prohibitions about contact with the foreign woman.

Maybe Anna sees me looking at Sasha while he is searching the dictionary to find the words to let me know he is still thinking about the connection between Russian roulette and Robbie Robertson's song "American Roulette." But the captain has forbidden the second engineer to lend the trawl crew his cassette player again.

When Anna watches me on the trawl deck, my face must have revealed to her that I am sometimes desperate for Sasha's smile, for his presence beside me and Alyosha on the port side of the stern ramp when we haul. We stand together, watching the hawser line tighten and wind back while we say the words we have memorized in each other's language. We know the words for sea and sky and work, and some words for how we feel. "Angry" and "hopeless" belong to Sasha. "Tired" and "sad" are mine.

I depend on Sasha to make me laugh, even without words. When we are drifting in the fog and the codend lies on the deck in tatters, Sasha might survey the damage, take off his hard hat and examine it as if he'd never seen it before, then put it on again, backwards, so the short rim looks like a Greek helmet, and assume a regal expression. I know he means to be Alexander of Macedon conquering the trawl deck's problems even before he announces this in Russian. I know, too, now, that when Anna looks around the main-deck door onto the trawl deck, she sees that I have come to need Sasha to get me through my time on *Provideniia*.

Anna seizes my hand one night when I am climbing up from the factory. "*Chai, chai,*" she shrieks. "Tea, Zhona, tea," and she leads me to the cabin she shares with Katya, the kitchen steward. Anna pushes me towards a stool beside the table, grabs her tin kettle and runs out, slamming the door behind her.

Anna's and Katya's cabin is also *Provideniia*'s laundry room, so there is room to move and light from extra portholes and the smell of ironed cotton. On the bulkhead beside each bunk are ragged-edged pictures of St Michael the Archangel and the Madonna, alongside magazine photographs of Russian movie stars dressed in gypsy costumes.

Anna flings open her own cabin door with the same force she uses on mine. In one hand she holds the kettle of water. Her other hand pushes the radio officer, who speaks some English, towards me. He sits down and explains that Anna wants to tell me a story. She has ten minutes to do it, he says sternly, before he goes on watch.

Anna shoves her immersion heater into the water in the kettle and begins. It is a joke, the radio officer translates. But Anna's face looks grave.

An old wolf is walking in the forest early one morning. The radio officer points westward. Perhaps in the country near the Carpathian Mountains. Anyway, the wolf's belly is full with the lamb he has stolen at dawn from the farmer's field below, and he feels satisfied with all the world. Then he spies a beautiful female wolf ahead of him on the winding trail.

She is beautiful, the radio officer repeats. Anna's hands fly, demonstrating the length of this woman wolf's fur, the curves of her flanks. Holding the tea tin and a spoon, hips swaying, Anna glides across her cabin to show how the female prances with her head in the air.

The old wolf is no longer satisfied with his full belly, or anything else in the world. He knows he won't be satisfied again until he has possessed the female. But how can this be arranged? She is young and lovely and her coat gleams. He is grey and gaunt and his fur is matted with the scars of old battles. Anna and the radio officer, a man of about fifty, both look thoughtful.

The young woman wolf has not seen the old one yet, though he is closer to her now. She is still prancing along, head lifted high. Quietly, the old wolf steps off the trail and hides himself in thick bushes.

Here, the story halts. Anna wants the Russian name of the bush translated. The radio officer looks helpless. Green and low and growing up high, he offers. Salal? Highbush cranberry? No. The old grey wolf hides himself in an unnamed bush.

"Cock-a-doodle-doo," he calls out from his hiding place in a high, crowing voice, "cock-a-doodle-doo!"

Anna flaps her arms to demonstrate how like a rooster he sounded.

The young wolf holds her stride, licks her lips, and turns her head. Her ears are pricked sharp. She looks around, then glides into the bush.

Anna still looks solemn. The radio officer looks slightly more interested. The water in the kettle has boiled and Anna pours our tea into chipped enamel cups. She and the radio officer stir four spoons of sugar into theirs. The old wolf pounces, overcomes the young beauty, and mounts her. The three of us consider this in silence.

Some time later, the old grey male is back on the trail. Now, he is truly satisfied with the world. "Yes," he says to himself with his head lifted high as he prances along, "when all is said and done, it's good to know a foreign language."

The radio officer smiles slightly, looks at his watch, and puts down his teacup. When Anna's door closes behind him, she and I look at each other. We are both quivering a little. "Cock-a-doodle-doo," we shriek at each other between bursts of helpless, sputtering laughter, "cock-a-doodle-doo!"

While we are laughing together, I am thinking Anna knows more about me, and my need for Sasha's smile and his admiration, as well as my occasional desperation at not being able to speak Russian, than I thought she or anyone else on *Provideniia* did.

We have enough fish for the night and *Provideniia* is drifting.

The captain's door has been locked since last night when he and the commissar and the chief engineer began drinking vodka.

On the bridge, we are drinking tea, Alexei, the chief mate, and I. Tiny wrinkled berries float in the cups and smell sweet and smoky. *Kamchatka* berries, Alexei calls them.

Katya says our chief cook is from Uzbekistan, where they put salt in their tea instead of sugar.

Viktor, the deck bo's'n, walks by the bridge windows and is outlined for a moment against the disappearing sun. Viktor and I are the only two on *Provideniia* with wildly curly hair and the only two who look awkward in the blunt haircuts Katya has been giving us all. He sees me through the port-side door and we both lift a hand to push back our hair, which makes the chief mate and Alexei laugh so much they have to walk out onto the deck to recover.

At 2100 on a calm sea with the sky still light this late in the season, we lost the codend. We have two other nets and the one we lost was old and worn, but none of this matters. Nor does it matter how the codend was fastened to the trawl lines or how many floats it carried, or even on which rock it may have snagged twenty-five fathoms below. What matters is that someone must bear the blame for the loss.

I am a long while learning this. In the hours before midnight, I have climbed up from the factory four times and seen only Mikhail Sergeyevich and Sasha and

Vitya and Alyosha fastening the grappling hook to the hawser line, then sliding it down the ramp. The four of them watch the line cut through *Provideniia*'s wake and sink. They wind the hook back on board after a while, change its position, let it go down the ramp again. They walk forward as far as the winch, pause, then return to the ramp and stare into the sea. They don't look at me standing by the scales and fish baskets, so I leave the deck and return to the factory. When I climb up and look again, they are behind the winch making tea, but their backs are still towards me.

After midnight, the ship is quiet. The factory is empty, the heading machines ground down to silence. The sluice of the cleanup hoses, mixed with the laughter of the crew, glad to be off shift early, has been punctuated by the slamming of cabin doors. Yuri, the foreman, and I have nodded good night to one another.

On the bridge deck, the captain has ceased yelling and gone to bed. *Provideniia* is making four knots along the same course she took when the codend sank. The chief mate is comparing the jagged sea bottom marked on the charts with the peaks showing on the paper sounder.

In my cabin, I move restlessly away from the paper-covered desk to look out on the empty passageway beyond my door, then to peer through the porthole. I should be contented. We are not fishing and there are no problems that involve me. No-one is refusing to understand me. No-one is being stubborn. Nothing can disturb my paperwork or my sleep before dawn.

When I walk out onto the storm bridge, Mikhail Sergeyevich looks up from the trawl deck below. For the first time since the codend was lost, he doesn't turn away from me. His face is set hard as he shrugs and holds out his empty hands. Perhaps I take a half-step towards the ladder. Instantly his right hand moves out in a flat, sideways gesture. Close your door so no-one knows you are not in there. I return to my cabin and shut the door, then walk back to the starboard ladder. These are the stairs without a handhold and Mikhail Sergeyevich comes partway up to meet me. With my hand on his shoulder, I climb down to the trawl deck.

Once I am wedged between Sasha and Vitya on the bench, Alyosha hands me a cup, filled not with coffee but with thin, sour wine that freezes, then burns as it goes down. None of the Russians looks at me. Their voices swirl around me while I drink my moonshine wine and say nothing. I am here beside them on the trawl deck and that is enough. When Mikhail Sergeyevich takes a pencil from his pocket, he looks at me at last and waits. I rip a page from my notebook and he writes columns of numbers, adds them, makes another column, subtracts and divides. Sasha, Alyosha, and Vitya examine the numbers. The paper goes back to Mikhail Sergeyevich and he hesitates, then hands it to me. The lists of numbers are in roubles. Why are we talking about thousands of roubles on the trawl deck? Alyosha points, and his finger follows the hawser line lying flat on the deck, leading down the stern ramp to the grappling hook below the sea, and at last I understand. The blame for losing the codend has been assigned. Mikhail Sergeyevich, Sasha, Alyosha, and Vitya will pay for it out of their fishing money.

I study each stern, closed face and learn nothing, so I lean forward, elbows on my knees and look at the slats beneath our boots instead. After a time, there is a sigh and Mikhail Sergeyevich drains his cup. Sasha murmurs a question and Mikhail nods without looking at him.

The strong wine is already blurring the edges around me, so the first notes of Sasha's guitar seem a natural part of the background until I remember I am sitting on the bench behind the winch on the Soviet ship *Provideniia*.

Sasha pays no attention to my surprise and picks at the chords for one tune, leaves it and starts another until he finds one we all know. When this song is over, I try to find out how he learned "The House of the Rising Sun," but they all look at me in astonishment and Vitya says this song is about the sorrows of gypsies, not about a man in despair in New Orleans.

Sasha plays a song he says is about a poet who disappeared in the thirties, another about a prisoner, then one written by a soldier in Afghanistan. We are all swaying and shifting in our places and drinking more and more wine. The Russians are singing, Mikhail Sergeyevich's voice always lower and later than the others. Vitya takes the guitar and plays something so fast his fingers can't keep up until he collapses in laughter and has to be propped upright by Alyosha.

When Sasha has the guitar again, he plays a rock song with words that twist his mouth into bitterness. Vitya gets up and staggers beyond the winch and begins to dance. He holds out his hand to beckon me to join him and I hold out mine to Mikhail Sergeyevich. We dance alone and then together, fast at first, then slowly, our steps matching the rise and fall of *Provideniia* through the sea. Alyosha dances with us when Mikhail Sergeyevich raises his hand to him, and Sasha plays rock-and-roll and gypsy music, then lays down the guitar and dances too. Our heads are thrown back to the black sky and the stars and there is no sound except the sea rushing past the hull and our own breathing and bursts of laughter.

When we are sitting on the bench again, with Alyosha leaning against the winch across from us, Sasha plays "The House of the Rising Sun" once more and I tell them some of the English words. New Orleans, New Orleans, the others murmur. Mikhail Sergeyevich raises his cup to toast New Orleans and we all drink. California, Florida, Texas ... Vitya's eyes are sparkling and Alyosha is smiling. White-line fever, I say, and there is a scramble to find the dictionary so I can explain. The need to go down the road. Restlessness.

We will all go. Down the road. Together. In a big Cadillac. No, a Mustang. Yes. Sasha will play the guitar for us all the way to California, to New Orleans and Texas. We will drink champagne and eat chocolates.

Golubaya mechta, Mikhail Sergeyevich says, heavenly blue dreams. Blue dreams are fantasies that will never come true.

The wine jar is almost empty. Mikhail Sergeyevich doles out the last of the liquor among our five cups and we drink without speaking. The guitar lies between

Sasha's feet. The faces of the Russians are softer now, sometimes revealing a touch of bewilderment that fades to weariness. We sit close together, even Alyosha is not standing for once, but crouching by our knees. Our eyes drift past one another, but I do not think any of us see the wires and ropes and machines that surround us. We are still dreaming, making *golubaya mechta*. Not the impossible fantasy of going down the road perhaps, but dreams that can come true only in a place and time we see no sign of yet. There is no real hope that Mikhail Sergeyevich will not have to leave his children for eight or ten months every year while he is at sea; that Sasha will ever own a car; that he or Vitya can afford to marry; that Alyosha will have all the books and raspberry jam he wants; that I will not be closer to Russian fishermen I will never see again than to any other men.

Provideniia never recovered the lost codend. Sasha never played the guitar on the trawl deck again. But every few days, one of us will say blue dreams, *golubaya mechta*, and smile, because something is settled among the five of us after this night, even if it is only that, on *Provideniia*, we know for certain that we are real.

There is a radio message about me leaving *Provideniia*, but because nothing else about the ship or the sea or the work changes, and because we are used to one another by now, no-one speaks of it.

If I am still hunched over my papers long after midnight, it may be that a hand will appear over my shoulder, set down a cup of black coffee and withdraw. Seldom do I turn quickly enough to see more than the edge of a blue shirt disappearing past my porthole, but I know whose hand this is.

Alyosha and I are the only ones on *Provideniia* who take coffee without sugar, and the only ones on the trawl deck who did not join the Komsomol when we were kids. One afternoon, Sasha and the other fishermen pantomimed themselves as eager young Komsomol boys for my entertainment. They sang the "Internationale," then saluted vigorously and spat. Mikhail Sergeyevich made a circle with his hands and grinned. Here we all are in the same place anyway, he meant. Alyosha shrugged.

If I look up from my desk in time to see Alyosha, I might beckon him into the circle of light inside my cabin. Alyosha will cross-hatch the first two fingers of each hand and lift them in front of his face. Prison bars. Prohibited. I know, but sometimes I wish to believe that Alyosha may sit on my bunk and drink his coffee while he regards me with his calm, pale grey eyes, and I motion to him anyway. He turns away and I go back to work and drink the coffee he brought me.

Every morning, I push open the heavy door to the trawl deck, jam on my hard hat while I stumble across the broken slats and begin to run to the stern for the first haul. My movements are still thickened with sleep when I fetch up against the port-stern deck rail beside Alyosha. Every morning, he carries two cups of coffee across the moving trawl wires and sets them on the cable drum at the stern.

If I climb up from the factory during the day and poke my head around the door to see if we are hauling, Alyosha holds up the coffee pot. I go back down to the heading machines and return in five or ten or fifteen minutes. I sit on the bench behind the winch and take some comfort from the dark strength of the coffee and from Sasha's and Vitya's shoulders hard against mine.

If the fishermen are net-mending, I drink my coffee propped against the trawl stashed on the starboard side. Alyosha's net knife weaves in and out of the mesh without pause. He wears a thin blue shirt with ripped sleeves and dark pants stuffed into black boots. Inside the boots, his feet are wrapped in rags. Few of the men on *Provideniia* have socks to work in.

If there is fog or rain, Alyosha wears the faded green liner from a Bering Sea coat. If it is sunny, he puts on a cocked hat made from a copy of *Izvestiia* five months old. His fair skin reddens anyway. His face is long and serious, falling into downward lines. Like almost everyone on *Provideniia*, he looks older than he is. Alyosha is thirty-six.

Alyosha knows when I wake at dawn or from my short afternoon sleep, and he puts the coffee on. He knows when I am hungry or tired or thirsty, and when the codend is too high for me to jump up on. But he will speak only Russian. Sasha uses the dictionary with great patience, searching out sequences of words and holding clumps of pages to make sentences for me. Mikhail Sergeyevich knows some English words and, like Vitya, he acts out the rest of what he wants to tell me, or draws in my notebook. But Alyosha will not use the dictionary, or act or draw pictures, he will only speak Russian, pouring out his words in a soft, liquid stream. After a time, I know the sense of what he is saying. You are pale, tired. Calm yourself. Eat. Sleep. Work is a wolf, always waiting to devour us. Alyosha has looked up only one word in the dictionary for me – *zhal*, compassion.

Alyosha checks the trawl deck before dinner and finds me crouched by a pile of salmon. He bends down and picks up a spring, hooks it onto the scale behind me. 2.5 kilograms, I write. Alyosha lays the salmon on my measuring board and I slash the belly. *Muzhskaya*, he mutters. Male. I switch the knife to my left hand and write again. He has another salmon hung up already. We turn to the scale at the same moment. Our arms and hands cross. Lift, weigh, record, measure, sex, record. Again and again.

We are both bloody to the elbows when the salmon are done. Alyosha runs salt water from the deck hose over my arms and murmurs something. I nod without knowing what he means. He speaks more urgently and mimics feeding himself. He flicks the water from his hands and takes my arm. Mikhail Sergeyevich, he says, and points and makes the eating gesture again. Mikhail Sergeyevich and the others are waiting for us in the crew's mess room where the door is always closed. From behind this door, I sometimes hear the commissar shouting. Now, Alyosha is holding the door open for me. Rows of faces look up. The men from the factory, from the engine room and the freezers and I are seeing each other differently. They have always been working when I've looked at them before. And I always eat in the officers' mess.

Alyosha's hand is on my shoulder, guiding me to the place Mikhail Sergeyevich, Vitya, and Sasha are saving for me. Sasha gets up to fetch me a bowl of thin, brown soup. My spoon clatters against the tin bowl and Mikhail Sergeyevich makes a soothing, rumbling noise in his throat.

"Family," Vitya suddenly announces. When we are sitting on the bench behind the winch, Vitya sometimes says mournfully, "Need woman, children." Yesterday, he printed "Chanel 5" on a scrap of paper torn from a block of black tea, squaring the letters so they looked Russian and I had to puzzle over them. "How much?" he asked. When I estimated the dollars, he began the conversion into fish, then roubles, and crumpled the paper.

Vitya makes toast for us on the trawl deck. For the length of a haul, about forty minutes, thick slabs of bread bubble slowly in butter, crowded into a dented frying pan set on the heating coil above the bench. Vitya turns the toast between changing gears on the winch.

Now, Sasha hands me a piece of bread and I break it in half and eat. Behind us, the bulkhead is covered with pictures of Lenin: Lenin's log-cabin childhood home; Lenin as a student; Lenin talking to men in uniforms and hard hats and sailors' gear; Lenin leaning on his desk and looking out at *Provideniia*'s crew eating dinner. Beside the pictures of Lenin is the list of daily production numbers for headed and gutted hake.

Slowly, I spoon up the soup and eat most of the bread. Vitya returns the empty bowl and brings it back filled with kasha and shreds of meat. I lift my soup spoon again, but Mikhail Sergeyevich holds up an imperious hand. Vitya rushes away to find a fork. My hand trembles less now and I get a forkful of kasha up to my mouth. The others watch carefully. When I chew in the necessary cautious fashion, they turn away satisfied. The kasha contains small stones now and then.

I work my way through half of the mound of kasha and some of the meat, depositing the fat bits on the rim of my bowl. Mikhail Sergeyevich scoops them into a paper napkin. I can't manage a dill pickle. Sasha has to eat the other half of my bread. I eat so slowly that everyone leaves the mess room except for the motormen playing trictrac and the four fishermen sitting with me. Alyosha pats the air. Calm. Calm. Mikhail Sergeyevich makes the pacifying sound in his throat again. Sasha takes my bowl away and we all leave the mess room together. I take the stairs down to the factory and they return to the trawl deck to finish mending the net. Alyosha turns at the door and raises his hand in a motion that is half farewell, half a blessing.

The night before I am to leave *Provideniia*, I ask Sasha to sing me the song about the young poet who disappeared in the thirties. When the song is done, Mikhail Sergeyevich clears his throat and rumbles through a few lines of Pushkin, repeating the poet's name before and after he begins to make certain I understand that much. Vitya elbows me. I look at each of their faces.

I cannot remember a word of Anna Akhmatova or Tsvetaeva. I cannot even remember what comes after the first line of the children's revolutionary song, "How many on our flesh have fattened." I cannot remember the name of the poet who wrote the lines I whisper, at last, to them, "Far and wide in anguish staring. My eyes grown stiff with tears will see."

"Aleksandr Blok," says Alyosha quite clearly. We finish this poem together, Alyosha in Russian and I in English, "Down the broad river slowly faring/ Christ in a skiff approaching me."

There was time enough to walk along the cramped space behind the line in the factory and touch each man on the shoulder, wait for him to lift his head and smile, or lean back to shout some words of farewell over the screech of the machines.

Time enough for Yuri, the foreman, to pull me into his cabin and thrust the last of *Provideniia*'s toffees, gathered and saved for me, wrapped in a newspaper bundle, into my hands.

There was time to listen to the captain's fears about what will happen when I'm gone, and to tell him there will be no problems with the fisheries patrol boat if *Provideniia* will only follow the procedures we all know now for the deck estimates and the logs and the by-catch. I look up our new word for him one last time. "Consult," as in to take advice from colleagues and subordinates to solve problems. The captain nods but he is staring out his window at the horizon when I leave his cabin.

There is just enough time to stuff my gear into the duffel bags. The camisoles and scarves and earrings are gone to Anna and Katya, but I still have more things than I had when I came on board. On top of my boots and jeans and books in the duffel bag are:

—one tin cup and one spoon from the trawl deck

—three rolls of gauze because Anna thinks it must be time for me to have my period

—thirty boxes of matches, because Vitya says they're the only things besides hake *Provideniia* has enough of

—ten packages of White Sea Canal cigarettes, the ones with the long cardboard filters, favoured by the factory crew because they can be clenched in the teeth and relit countless times. Besides, they are the cheapest cigarettes available and the White Sea Canal was built by slave labour also. Sasha points out you can twist the cardboard tube a certain way and whistle through it.

—one aerosol can, possibly floral room spray, from the boy with the huge eyes who works in the engine room

—one rusted, heavy-duty S-shaped hook, made for me by the mechanic after the fish basket with fifty kilograms of cod in it slipped off the scale hook and hit me in the mouth

—two wooden spoons, painted with flowers on a black background, from Vlodya Nicolaievich, night foreman in the factory

—one baby's rattle, wrapped in a flowered hanky, from Irina, the doctor

—one bottle of vitamin C, from Yuri, day foreman in the factory

—one tin of instant coffee, from the captain, along with the news that the Soviets invented instant coffee

—one bottle of valerian drops, for the nerves, from Katya

—one Russian-English dictionary, published in Moscow, 1973, from Mikhail Sergeyevich

—one Russian rock-music tape, first and last songs chopped off, from Sasha

—one lipstick, used, from Anna

—one pair of earrings from Peru, the favourites among all of Katya's earrings

—one book of poems by Aleksandr Blok, from Alyosha

—three meal sacks

—one pair of black bo's'n's pants, produced from ship's stores by Viktor, the deck bo's'n, after the captain ordered him to find something for me to wear because my laundry had not come back in time

—one Soviet worker's award, from the captain, lettered by the third officer, praising my conscientious work and "active assistance" to the Soviet Union and requesting peace and friendship between our nations

—one hammer and sickle flag, never used, bright red as blood

—one hammer and sickle flag, flown from the day *Provideniia* left Petropavlovsk until the day I left, faded and frayed

—one calendar commemorating the voyages of Vitus Bering, from the captain.

Now, I am on the boat deck, wearing the black high-top runners for transferring at sea, and there is no more time. Viktor is pushing my bags up the ladder into the lifeboat. The chief mate is explaining that he ·cannot order the ports in the boat opened because of the huge swell, even though he understands that I hate to be shut inside without light or fresh air.

Anna and Katya are weeping luxuriously. The night shift in the factory and the freezer crew and the motor-men are reaching awkwardly for my hands.

The third officer is ready to steer the lifeboat, and Alyosha and Vitya, who will be the crew, are already inside. Sasha hands Mikhail Sergeyevich my life jacket and Mikhail buttons me into it. Both of their faces are stern and closed again, but their eyes meet mine.

I climb the ladder and Alyosha is there to help me make the long drop to the bottom. Vitya closes the port and the lifeboat lowers into the sea.

Diesel fumes fill the air and we climb and fall towards the Canadian dragger standing off *Provideniia*'s bow. Alyosha sits beside me for the first time and Vitya hands me a length of net twine fastened into a bracelet with codend knots.

My feet are clinging to the rounded top of the lifeboat rolling in the swell alongside the Canadian boat. The noise of the sea and both boat engines roars in my ears. We crash against the dragger's steel hull every time we drop down with the swell.

The third officer has hold of one arm and Alyosha has the other. He is saying something to me, but I can't hear him. He looks at the third officer, who shouts a translation, "Don't be afraid, Zhona," and I shout back, "I am not afraid." The three of us crouch as the lifeboat lifts again in the swell, then I jump, thrust up and out by the strength of my knees and their arms, and land safely on the deck of the Canadian boat.

When I remember *Provideniia*, I remember that we were all afraid. The glass wall between the Russians and me at the beginning of our voyage was thickened and blurred by fear.

I was afraid of their contempt for a foreign woman with an easier life than theirs. Most of all, I feared the temptation to punish them by turning their mistakes and their stubbornness over to the fisheries patrol boat because they refused, for what seemed like a long time, to see that they made my days hard and lonely with their mistrust.

Perhaps the Russians feared me because they thought I would be contemptuous of them, not because of the shabbiness of their ship or the rags instead of socks or the commissar's bullying or the stones in the kasha, but because of their own shame in believing for so long that this life was all that was possible for them.

Maybe they were afraid because they learned from me that they have the power to make someone other than themselves suffer.

When I wake in the night now, and there is no engine noise, no sound of the sea rushing past the porthole, I think, sometimes, of *Provideniia*. She is likely on the Bering Sea. Because we know each other a little, the Russian crew and I, and are not afraid of each other, I am content to imagine them on their ship, or in Petropavlovsk, or wherever they are, and to hope and pray for them. I know that, now and then, they do this for me.

RADIO SILENCE

It is difficult to imagine the land once it has disappeared and there is only the sea, and now it is hard to remember the truth about the foreign ships.

One short scene, morning or late afternoon. Fog or sun. It doesn't matter. I will rush into the radio room with some papers: certainly yesterday's catch reports and the charting for the hake samples, possibly also the cumulative tonnage for rockcod by-catch (minimal) or a note about the fillet conversion rate in the factory. I will grab the handset, which will immediately turn slippery from my sweat, and check to be sure I am on 2182, the calling channel. At the time I won't know that my lips are already moving, silently reciting a litany, "... Sierra Quebec India Juliet calling...."

There I am, standing, not touching anything except the handset because my jacket and boots are crusted with hake scales. The radio officer will regard me with what I think is disdain. He may point to his own cheek to indicate I have blood on mine. I might get as far as pressing the transit button, creating a blank space in the static buzz in which I can speak. Possibly I will open my mouth. Then I will notice the clock, set to Warsaw or Moscow time, is on the hour or the half-hour. More likely the radio officer will tap his watch, a little pleased, I assume, that I was about to make a mistake.

Radio silence is required from 00 to 03 minutes and from 30 to 33 minutes every hour on 2182 to allow distress calls from distant ships to be heard.

At first, the empty air will seem truly silent. The banging of the door to the trawl deck below and the rush of the sea pouring past our hull will emphasize this quiet. Some days, the blurred static still present on the empty channel will thicken, then recede and push forward again, as if breathing. The radio officer and I will bend over the transmitter and I will close my eyes to hear more clearly. The ship rolls hard and the transmitter lurches against its lashings, making me thrust out my hand and turn my face away. The radio officer never moves.

The hardest part is trying not to want to hear a voice, thinned by distance and distorted by the radio, calling to be found.

We cannot hear the tick of the clock over the main engines, but its hands have almost crossed the three-minute silence. The radio officer is already looking out his window again, bored. The scratch of sound on 2182 settles to a faint rise and fall, noticeable only because it is slightly out of rhythm with the slower roll of the ship.

STILL A SAILOR'S STORY

Ever since Nikolai and Boris discovered that I know what happened to Sergei Kirov in 1934, and that I remember where Marina Tsvetaeva is buried, they have been convinced I can understand Russian when I try.

The two of them are throwing Russian words at each other with great passion when I walk onto the trawl deck. But the fishermen's gathering place behind the winch is only a way station for me this morning, a pause between working on the logbooks up in the captain's cabin and counting fish in the factory down below. I am thinking about the conversion test I may have time to run on the heading machine before the next haul, so I lean on the arm of Boris's bo's'n's chair and register no more than his and Nikolai's disdain for the subject of their conversation.

Boris gets up to give me the chair, holding out his hand as he does so. I find the Russian-English dictionary, crumpled and damp, in my jacket pocket and wipe it on my sleeve before I hand it to him. "Animals," he says gravely after a moment's search through the pages. He adds a word or two in Russian, then sweeps a huge hand towards the crew's quarters on the other side of the bulkhead behind us. He pinches his thumb and forefinger together. Only a few animals.

My face must look exceptionally vacant. "*Schayhoff*," Nikolai says severely, but this means nothing to me. Nikolai crouches, makes a circle of his hands, and pantomimes looking through it. Under his slightly exasperated gaze, I consider the clues: animals; a view through a circle; and Boris's gesture towards the quarters for about fifty men with one cabin shared between my dear Valentina, who is patient about the hake scales and spilled coffee on the floor under my desk, and Julia, the ship's laundrywoman, who regards me with cheerful contempt.

Then I remember another crew on another ship, and other circles:

We were casting lots. There were twenty-two of us who, having stood watch, were now at liberty. Out of this number only two were to have the luck of enjoying a rare spectacle. On this particular night the honeymoon cabin was occupied, but the wall of the cabin had only two holes at our disposal. One of them I myself had made with a fine saw, after boring through with a corkscrew: the other had been cut out with a knife by one of my comrades. We had worked at it for more than a week.

I leap up, dislodging the worn Bering Sea coat which cushions the chair. "Chekhov," I shriek at Boris and Nikolai, "'A Sailor's Story.'"

"*Schay-hoff*," Nikolai tells me, "no Check-hov." But he and Boris are satisfied that I have at last understood what they were telling me, and we settle back, the two of them on either side of me, leaning on the arms of the chair. Nikolai's body slumps a little, then straightens. Boris sighs.

After a time, *Arctic Ocean* passes our starboard quarter towing a full codend for us. Boris leans over and flips our hard hats down from their hooks behind the bo's'n's chair. With infinite gentleness, Nikolai sets mine on my head, and the three of us step onto the trawl deck together.

LANA JANINE

MARINE FORECAST, OFFSHORE BOWIE. NORTHERN SECTION. WINDS SOUTHEASTERLY 30 TO GALES 40 KNOTS SHIFTING TO EASTERLY 35 OVERNIGHT. PERIODS OF RAIN. SEAS 3 TO 4 METRES. OUTLOOK: WINDS RISING AGAIN TO GALE FORCE SOUTHEAST.

At Nahwitti Bar outside Goletas Channel at the top end of Vancouver Island, a southeast wind pushes against the tide, churning a few whitecaps out of the chop. *Lana Janine* leans towards the land she is leaving behind, picks herself up and falls seaward, all the while moving ahead. The heavy mast that once stabilized her has been removed to make space for blackcod gear, so now she rolls, wood hull creaking, on the smallest sea.

Lana Janine, who used to be the *Mary Lou*, was built in 1946 and 1947 at Lynch Shipyard in San Diego,

1,200 sea miles south of here. 36.58 metres in length, her certificate of registry says 255.41 gross tons. Stem: Raked. Stern: Fantail. Build: Caravel.

The boat was made for Mexican sardine and tuna fisheries, but she has passed through many hands and this is not her first northern voyage. *Lana* has fished halibut in the Bering Sea, and, in another season with other owners, she has lain on the bottom by the dock in Port Simpson up the British Columbia coast. Now, carrying a captain, six crew men, and me, she is making her way to Bowie Seamount to fish blackcod with traps. Bowie Seamount, just inside Canadian waters 200 sea miles offshore in the north Pacific, is an underwater volcanic mountain. Blackcod feed and thrive in its steep, shadowed canyons.

Lana Janine is ploughing out of Goletas Channel to the open water off Cape Scott on the same course sailed 200 years ago by a schooner whose home port was the Spanish naval base at San Blas, Mexico. The schooner's captain was Dionisio Alcalá Galiano, who was circumnavigating Vancouver Island in the *Sutil*, accompanied by Captain Cayetano Valdés in the *Mexicana*. Both men were exploring the coast of British Columbia for a northwest passage to the Atlantic.

Galiano named the channel "*Goletas*" after the Spanish word for schooner, and wrote in his journal, "The wind strengthened to the extent that we had to lie with the mainsail double reefed, and at times with such strong gusts that we could not carry even this sail. We intended to pass the time in the shelter of the land. Considering that if, as it appeared, the wind continued in the south we would be set far to the north, lose the shelter of the land, and move away from our destination, we decided to return to the channel."

The *Sutil* and the *Mexicana*, both bearing masts and riggings which Galiano thought were of poor quality, stayed four days "in the shelter of the land" until the wind dropped enough to allow them to round Cape Scott and continue down the west coast of Vancouver Island to Nootka. *Lana Janine*, pitching and staggering on not much more than the Beaufort scale's definition of a fresh breeze – "17 to 21 knots. Moderate waves, taking a more pronounced long form. Many white horses are formed. Chance of some spray" – slopes on through the night across Queen Charlotte Sound. In the morning, on deck, my round pocket mirror reflects a white face, and, over my shoulder, Cape St James at the bottom of the Queen Charlotte Islands to the east. Our course is 299 degrees true now, northwest to Bowie Seamount, and the ridged blue coast of the Charlottes fades into the sky as the day moves on.

Thirty-two hours beyond Nahwitti Bar, the fishermen on *Lana Janine*'s tilting deck are baiting wire-mesh traps with frozen fish scraps. They clip the heavy traps to a mile of line unreeling from the stern drum, and fasten both ends of the line or "string" to numbered floats flying black flags to mark commercial fishing gear. The string of traps will soak sixteen, eighteen, twenty hours in the darkness 1,200 fathoms below. The fish feeding at the deepest levels will be blind.

Branches of pink and white coral and crumbled lava fragments will snag on the wire mesh while the drifting scent of bait lures a few rougheye and other red rockfish, tanner crabs, and king and queen crabs, along with blackcod, into the traps' cone-shaped mouths.

Ten strings soaking, fifty-five traps to a string. 2.75 to 3.25 kilograms average weight per fish. Six or seven pounds. Fifteen hundred pounds of headed, gutted, scraped-clean blackcod to a tote. Four totes to a freezer load.

Each of my sample trays has preserving solution and space for a hundred pairs of otoliths. Otoliths are a fish's ear bones, tiny bone plates set on either side of the brain cavity and marked with minute ridges which can be examined to tell the age of the fish.

The decks are awash with blood and sea water twenty hours a day. If we look up from our work, we see clouds collecting at the edge of the sky, appearing as hills that, in turn, suggest the chance of valleys.

The weather is fair enough, grey and cold but seldom blowing more than thirty knots. Still, we are forever climbing up one side of *Lana*'s slanted deck, then bracing ourselves for the steep-angled descent down the opposite edge of the roll. *Lana Janine* rolls on a following sea and when she is headed into swells. She rolls wallowing in the waves' trough, and riding high in the spray. She rolls when the main engines are running, and when they are shut down. She rolls on both rising and falling seas, and she rolls on no sea at all, on flat calm water. Only one of the men speaks against her for this. Roll then, you bloody whore, he says. Roll your guts out.

She staggers from side to side to catch the balance she lost when her great, heavy mast was taken from her. Trembling and hesitating on the easiest sea has become *Lana Janine*'s continuing revelation of her vulnerability. She cannot help herself. The latches on every one of her port and starboard doors are loosened now, from the strain of leaning.

After midnight, when we stop hauling so the men can rest a few hours, *Lana Janine*'s main engines are shut off, allowing her to drift. We sleep in bunks built abeam, which means our heads suffuse with blood, then our feet jam into the bulkheads all through the short night. The only bunks made fore and aft are the wooden boxes crammed into the forepeak. These crates, filled with machine parts now, were beds for the Mexican fishermen who were *Lana Janine/Mary Lou*'s first crews on the Gulf of Mexico and Baja California tuna fishery. The Mexican fishermen left another reminder of their presence on the upper deck.

The door by the ladder leading to the wheelhouse is inset with a blue glass cross. Beyond the sacks of potatoes and cases of root beer and Coke stacked in the tiny cabin is an altar. Beneath a hardwood arch, Mary is flanked by the figures of her grown son, who delicately indicates his bleeding heart, and Joseph, holding the boy Jesus in his arms. Smaller statues of a black-robed nun carrying a crucifix and a tonsured monk with a child complete the company.

During the dead hours of the night, *Lana Janine* dips and turns, parting the sea as she drifts so that it pours past her stern sounding like a waterfall halting, then beginning again. The chapel door loosens on the starboard slide, banging into my sleep. When I get up and step out onto the deck in my bare feet, the sea under a moon-streaked sky flows away on either side of the boat like a field of grain stirred by the wind.

Lana heels over hard, so I barely manage to catch the chapel door before it slams one more time. Against the shadowed bulkhead at the back of the little cabin, the Madonna's white plaster face has become dark enough to make her Mexico's Virgin of Guadalupe. Tonight, while the boat continues to lunge, alone on the ocean, the figure of the woman in the chapel seems to be *Lana Janine* herself, our lady of the north Pacific, madonna of mercy on the seamount, our sanctuary on a sea where there is no other help for us. She is not troubled by clouds masquerading as mountains, or by distant, unreal valleys. She will bear us home, despite the desperate motion of her hull, and the long curve of sea until the land rises before us again. The rusted rosary dangling from the Virgin's hand sways wildly as *Lana Janine* leans deeply to port. Moonlight washes the pale blue roof of the chapel. I put my shoulder to the door, pushing hard to secure the catch, then return to my own cabin to lie down and surrender again to the familiar, forgiven, head-to-foot sliding which slowly turns to sleep.

THE MASTER OF
THE *HALNIAK*

Swam to me the green fish,
Flew to me the white seagull,
I was gay, and bold, and wicked,
And never knew I was happy.

—Anna Akhmatova
"By the Seashore"

The gap between the *Delfin* and the cargo ship *Halniak*
narrowed until I could see that the master of the *Halniak* was smaller and jauntier than our bulky captain.
As the deck crews let down the bumpers and fastened
the lines, he looked down on them, then across at me,

with one fierce, bright eye. The other eye was covered with a black patch.

Delfin, a 2500-ton Polish stern trawler, was tying alongside the *Halniak* to off-load frozen hake and fish meal. While my captain and I watched the aft holds being opened, he spoke of the monotony that cargo ship captains suffer without the excitement of fishing. Diversion was necessary to them, he explained, no matter its dangers. For example, not a month earlier, a woman shot the master of the *Halniak* during a diversion in Montevideo. The bullet had grazed his eye.

What did the woman look like? I wanted to ask. Nothing like me, I knew. Certainly, she would have worn a dress. Red, I thought. After the gun went off, she would have sunk back into her chair, horrified at what she had done. Later, she would thank God the bullet wound was no worse. But when the *Halniak* sailed, she might perhaps have watched from a window table in some bar overlooking Montevideo harbour, a little pleased that she had left her mark on the master.

Safe in Mayne Bay, deep inside Barkley Sound, the man with the eye patch leaned on his deck rail and began to talk to the captain in Polish. The joined shadows of the ships darkened the water, and the sun had already crusted the hake scales on the knees of my jeans. Pallet boards stacked with cartons swung on the winches. The green smell of the land blew across the ship while I stared at the shore, wondering how I had forgotten about trees for forty days.

"Joanna," the captain said, "this master invites I, and also you, to visit his ship." I looked up to the bridge of the *Halniak*. The small man bowed. I went to my cabin to see if the chief engineer had fixed the hot water. He had, so I washed my hair in the leaking sink, anticipating the small diversion of visiting a ship where no-one knew or cared about fishing regulations.

On the boat deck, the captain and Kazik, our trawl bo's'n, stood beside me. At our feet, a rope ladder knotted with wooden slats lopped down from the *Delfin* and up to the *Halniak*. The captain pushed me gently towards the ladder. "I come also," he said, "after business." He made a writing gesture in the air.

Kazik climbed down to the U-shaped curve at the bottom of the ladder, turned to find a foothold on the other side of the loop, and moved quickly up onto the *Halniak*. Without looking at the loosely bagged safety net or the water below, I followed him. He held my elbow delicately, steering me through passageways lined with familiar brown linoleum. He knocked on an inside door, released my elbow and turned to leave as the door opened.

The man wearing a patch sat at the head of a long table. He stood up to kiss my hand and pulled out the chair next to him. I sat. One dark eye stared at me. "*Ochmistrzu*," he called, and his chief steward appeared.

"Master. Miss Joanna." The steward waited.

"Vodka?" the master asked.

"Coffee," I answered.

I drank my coffee. The master drank his vodka. He moved his chair closer, smiling as he watched me eat four of his chocolates filled with the white cream the Poles call bird's milk. I bit each chocolate in half so he could examine them, but I didn't find the egg, the one with a yellow centre.

"*Ochmistrzu* ..." The chief steward came in again. This time, he listened to a lengthy order in Polish.

"The master wishes to say your eyes begin to speak yes to him."

"They do not." I set my coffee glass down hard in its saucer. The master smiled and my face burned. I wished I were sitting at the plywood table in my own cramped and airless cabin. I wished for a storm and thirty tons of hake on the trawl deck. "I must return to the *Delfin*," I said, "business." The two men spoke to each other in Polish again.

"The master says Jackie needs to see you for one moment only." The steward placed his hand over his heart. I cared nothing about who Jackie might be, only that he offered an escape from the master's smile. I followed the steward along passageways that smelled of bleach and shone with new white paint, folding in a finger for every turn we made so I could find the starboard ladder again.

A door was flung open. Inside, Jackie flew about the steward's cabin in a yellow blur. He hovered above a tightly tucked bunk, danced on a photograph of the pope, and lighted on a vine trailing past the porthole.

"You are the first woman Jackie has seen since Montevideo," the steward said, but I paid him no mind. Jackie's quick brightness enchanted me. More than white paint and bleach-scented air, more even than bird's milk chocolates, Jackie was a contradiction to the *Delfin*'s rusted steel and hills of grey hake.

The steward chirped until Jackie flew to his finger. Carefully, he transferred him to my hand. Fluorescent yellow feathers lay along the tiny body in perfect trim. Minute black markings outlined a neck the circumference of a cigarette. The bird and I both trembled. I saw that my nails were rimmed with grey. Jackie tipped his head to one side and appeared to regard me with hope.

"He cannot drink the water from the ship," the steward said. "He drinks only with the master and me. From here." His hand guided Jackie to my mouth, and the small, sharp beak pecked dryly at my lips. I opened my mouth. The steward watched closely. When Jackie was satisfied, I handed him back and asked for the ladder.

In the morning, the sun, which had been a comforting warmth offshore, bore down on the *Delfin*. The winches ground constantly, but the men loading the pallets and cargo slings moved slowly through the heat on the trawl deck outside my cabin. I sat at the table beneath my porthole, writing one word at a time to describe the biological sampling I had done at sea, lifting my head often to catch a breeze. Kazik came to my door and pointed up to the bridge: "*Kapitan*."

I edged past the open hold and made my way up top, determined not to answer any of the captain's questions about my visit to the *Halniak*, nor to ask him why he had not come after me as he had promised he would.

The bridge had become strange, static territory now that the voices on the radio and the ticking of the steering indicator were silenced, and the blurred bands of fish and feed no longer moved across the sounder screen. The captain asked no questions. Instead, he waved towards the green shore beyond the glare bouncing off the bridge windows. "The master of the *Halniak* makes an excursion for us," he said, "to the land." I looked at the captain's feet and saw that he had replaced his shipboard sandals with shoes. This time, he meant to come with me. He watched my face as I remembered the trees. "Good," he said. "To the lifeboat."

The master, the chief steward, who held a bulging flight bag on his knees, and *Delfin's* doctor were waiting for us in the port lifeboat. A young mechanic, his face leached pale from the heat of the engine room, had already fired up the motor in a burst of black smoke. When the captain and I were settled, the lifeboat swung out from its davits and dropped to the water.

I sat beside the mechanic, my face turned away from the others, grateful that the sea was near to me again, its surface only gently ruffled now, not falling away into the long, offshore swells. The doctor and the steward chattered together in Polish. My captain, large in the bow, made no comment as the master of the *Halniak* steered wide, lurching circles around

Mayne Bay. After several false passes, we landed at a logging company dock posted with a sign forbidding anyone to tie there.

On the narrow beach beside the dock, a man in shorts tended two barbecues, setting steaks on one and hamburgers on the other. A woman sat nearby in a folding chair while two children played on an inner tube at the water's edge. They watched in silence as we set off into the bush, led by a small, staggering pirate. The mechanic stayed behind to mind the lifeboat.

The path was so overgrown we had to walk in single file. Behind me, the doctor called out excitedly. "He saw a nightingale," the chief steward reported from farther back in the procession.

"I'm afraid we have no nightingales in Canada," I told him.

"Impossible," was his reply.

The salal and alder leaves were filmed with dust from the path. I breathed in the scent of dry, heated earth and gave up wondering where we were going. Deadfall spruce trees, blackberry and huckleberry branches, sprawling cedar roots, all these caused us to bunch together, our bodies crushed into the undergrowth while we examined each discovery.

The master urged us on. He wished to reach the river, the steward explained, but I did not believe there was a river.

We walked out of the bush onto a bed of dry stones. Weeks without rain had diminished the river to a creek. We camped beside it.

The steward opened his flight bag, laid a white cloth on the rocks, and set out vodka, glasses, and bread with sausage. The master filled our glasses and proposed a toast to the land and the river, small as it was. We drank, then he leaned on his elbow, looked up at me, and said something in Polish which made my captain close his eyes. "Shut up, master," the chief steward said severely. I turned away, looking along the river bank for a black bear who would devour all the Poles, then return to the forest, leaving me to follow him if I wished.

The master drooped. Still holding his glass of vodka, he leaned over the creek and uttered a command. His steward knelt beside him, splashing water ferociously over the bent head until the master sat up looking sombre and drained his glass.

The two captains, as much at ease propped against a log as they were in their own cabins, began to drink more vodka and speak only to each other. The doctor drifted away among the trees to search for nightingales. I wandered upstream, wanting to believe I could continue climbing to the mountain where the river began, leaving the master of the *Halniak* and the sea behind me forever. The chief steward followed me at a distance. When I let him catch up at the first bend in the river, he said he had been ordered to protect me from the wilderness.

I walked ahead of him again and found a cutoff pool fingertip to elbow deep. Coho fry and stickleback flickered in the pool's shadows. I showed the silvery little fish to the chief steward when he came up, but after he had admired them, he reminded me that we must turn back. The master would want his ship soon, he said.

This was true. The vodka was finished and my captain was dozing, but the small figure standing by him gazed anxiously downstream as if expecting his ship to be making way in the shrunken river. The doctor had returned without a nightingale, but with a handkerchief full of rosehips. The steward collected the heel of bread and the empty bottles and we walked the narrow path through the bush again. We were all silent this time, brushing aside the branches and runners that crossed our bodies, coming out at last to Mayne Bay. The ships lay safe in the centre of a flat blue circle of sea. The picnickers were gone and only the mechanic lay sunning himself on the dock beside the lifeboat. He steered a straight course to *Halniak*'s port side. No-one turned to look back at the land. It was no longer ours.

The excursion to the shore had exhausted me. I planned to sleep away the heat of the late afternoon so I could work on my report about *Delfin*'s cargo through the evening. Kazik would come on shift at eight that night and I would get him to take me down to the freezer holds. The cartons of frozen fish were almost done and hundreds of bags of fish meal were being off-loaded, meaning the end of transshipping was in sight.

The captain came to my door. "To *Halniak*," he said, ignoring my nightgown. "Dinner and farewell." I didn't want to tell him I was weary of the master making me feel like an awkward girl again. I was afraid to refuse the dinner invitation without an explanation, then live with his disapproval when I still had to work at sea with him for days to come. I shut my door, washed the dust from my hands and face, and dressed in the shirt and jeans I had just taken off.

Once I was sitting in the master's cabin, he insisted that my captain remind me I was now the queen of two ships. Along with the vodka, there was a bottle of Russian champagne on the table. The chief steward apologized so profusely for its warmth that I felt obliged to drink it. Both captains and the officers from the *Halniak* applauded.

Dinner was quickly over and cleared away. We drank a toast to fair voyages, we drank to Poland, to Canada, to Mayne Bay, to me. Someone proposed we advance to the northwest and conquer Russia. The steward came in with a guitar, saying he would play only the old music, songs about sailors and gypsies, about love and sorrow. The others sang with him until a tear leaked from beneath the black patch. The steward switched to a polka. The master got up, bowed, over-balanced, and could not save himself. He lay on the floor of his cabin with his hand under his cheek, smiling like a tired child. The largest of his officers picked him up and carried him to bed.

The polka continued. I danced with my captain, then with the other men. When the music stopped, their laughter and the noise of clinking glasses rose around me and the floor of the cabin rolled away from my feet, carrying me as if it were the sea. I floated towards the door. "Miss Joanna, Miss Joanna," they called, and put another glass of champagne into my hand.

Kazik was suddenly there in the crowded cabin, asking our captain some question in his quiet voice. "*Tak*, yes," the captain answered as he poured vodka for him. Kazik upended his glass and smiled a little.

"*Delfin*," I whispered to him and he took hold of my elbow again to guide me towards the door, along the passageways to the ladder. He looked into my eyes and raised his clenched fists. Hold tight with your hands, he meant. He stood back and I began the journey.

On the deck, the first awkward crouch and turn, still grasping the stanchions. Send down the right foot and search for the wooden slat to hold it. Now the left. Kazik and I are alone amidships, the voices of the crew working forward are muffled and distant. His shadow blacks out the deck light above the ladder. My foot slides into the air once, making the unbalanced ladder sway and my body swing to one side with it. My hands are wrapped so tightly around the ropes the skin on my fingers aches, but Kazik, above me on the *Halniak*, makes no sound until I stop far down the ladder, ready to turn and reach one hand to the other side of the loop. He calls out sharply. Not yet, he must mean. I move down one step, then another, until my weight brings the far side of the ladder closer to me. I turn, and am only for an instant spread sideways, a foot on either side of the loop. The taste of champagne is still in my mouth, but I am not the queen of two ships any more, and the rungs are steady under my feet as I climb up *Delfin*'s rust-streaked hull to the deck.

In my cabin, the breeze had cooled the air for the first time in days. The tide tugged at the ship, making the rubber bumpers below my porthole shriek softly, then subside. Before I slept, I wondered if the master of the *Halniak* ever dreamed, ever felt clumsy or foolish, or only amused by his diversions.

On the bridge in the morning, the third officer plotted our course from Mayne Bay through Imperial Eagle Channel, out of Barkley Sound and back to sea. The chart for offshore waters and the joint-venture fishing logs were set out again.

I stood beside the captain watching Kazik and the fishermen lay the codend on the trawl deck. *Halniak*'s men were already standing by the tie-up lines although there was no sign of the master on their bridge. I was glad of his absence, then ashamed of myself. He had given me bird's milk chocolates and Jackie's brightness. He had taken me to the land and found the river I did not believe in, then he had diverted me with music and champagne and dancing. It might be that he had expected, or perhaps only hoped, that I would lie down in his bed, but he had not been surprised or less generous when I had not. I had given him nothing, not so much as a smile, and I didn't want to be reminded of my parsimony.

Halniak's first officer fastened a small bag to a line and threw it onto our bridge wing. The captain handed the bag to me. I opened it reluctantly, but it contained only the bills of lading for the cargo. An unimaginably long time ago, when we first began transshipping to the *Halniak*, I had insisted I needed these documents to check the tonnage we off-loaded. I shoved the papers into my hip pocket as the captain stepped forward to shout down to Kazik. The amidships lines were released, then the bow. *Delfin* hesitated before she began to slide away from the *Halniak*, held only by her stern lines.

The master of the *Halniak*, pale and severe, stepped onto his bridge deck. He looked as if he had been born wearing the black patch. I should have sent over a thank-you note in the bag, I thought. The steward could have translated it. On paper, I could have managed to be warm-hearted. The master snapped his fingers and the steward appeared beside him with the guitar. He struck the first chords.

"My Bonnie lies over the ocean," the master sang across the gap between us, thickening the words until they sounded Polish. "My Bonnie lies over the sea. Oh bring back, bring back, bring back my Bonnie to me, to me."

I looked up at him. The grim mouth quirked at the corners, then tightened again. I started to laugh. I waved to him with both hands. I laughed until my knees loosened and I had to clutch the deck rail to keep from falling. The stern lines were let go. The main engines started up. *Delfin* moved farther and farther away from the *Halniak*, and still I laughed while the master grinned, waving back, a wide, across-the-body, arm-stretching wave, still visible at three or four cables' distance.

The department of fisheries encourages foreign ships to transship offshore now, not in Mayne Bay. We tie alongside the cargo ship and drift, rolling out of time with each other in heavier seas, straining the lines between us. The winches swing loaded pallet boards back and forth. I check the holds, insist that we note the cartons and bags lost overboard, look at bills of lading when we are done. The ladder linking the ships is always there, but I seldom use it.

I never saw the *Halniak* again, although she entered Canadian waters this past hake season, taking fish from the *Kantar*, the *Parma*, and the *Otol*. I was working on other ships, smiling more easily, laughing, and sometimes raging, more than I had before I knew the master of the *Halniak*.

OUT OF SIGHT OF LAND

*Both Homer and the sea: all things are moved by
    love;
To whom shall I pay heed? Homer here is silent
And the dark sea thunders, eloquent,
And rumbling heavily, it breaks beneath my bed.*

—Osip Mandelstam
"Insomnia. Homer. Tautly swelling sails."

Morning

The Polish fishing ship *Jan Łaski*, 122 days at sea, is
trawling for hake in the early morning fog off Canada's
west coast. *Jan Łaski*'s captain, who is sixty years old
and thinks he has forgotten the village where he was
born because it disappeared during the war, has been
peering into the radar screen's black rubber viewing
hood for an hour.

The radar shows a moving point farther out to sea. According to Tofino Traffic, this is the bulk carrier *Suruga Maru*, bound for Yokohama at eighteen knots, no course change. The captain switches the radar range and a point is now displayed on his port side, closer this time. He clicks his teeth in irritation and orders the helmsman to increase speed, then turn five degrees to starboard. At home in Gdynia, his wife corrects the teeth-clicking habit, but no-one mentions it here, and he believes he doesn't make this sound when he is on the ship.

In the radio room, the transmitter spits out soft static. "Gdynia, Gdynia, Gdynia," the radio officer recites, "*Jan Łaski*, Sierra Bravo Juliet November." He glances at the clock set seven hours ahead to Polish time, then resumes his effort to reach the Gdynia radio operator so the captain can call his wife at home. The radio officer swallows as he pauses to allow a reply from Poland, tasting the memory of cherry-jam-filled *paczek* from the stall on the square in Bydgoszcz. He moves the handset away from his mouth, closing his eyes so he can remember how the river water in the Vistula-Noteć Channel smells young and green and faintly sour.

In Gdynia, it is mid-afternoon and the captain's wife is waiting for the phone to ring. She has decided to tell her husband that their younger son is drinking again. If necessary, she will remind the captain of last year's voyage, when he called about the shopping she wanted done in Vancouver, and revealed that he had forgotten the boy's age. The captain will not tell his wife anything about *Jan Łaski*, nor will she ask. They both believe that the enclosed, foreign world of the ship has nothing to do with their life together, or with Poland.

Below decks in the factory, a thick stream of hake flows towards the man who sorts the fish onto conveyor belts feeding the filleting machines. The man looks over his shoulder out the porthole close to the water line and sees that the fog has lifted a little, leaving a band of grey sea visible. After a moment, he cannot recall what he has just seen. He turns and looks out of the porthole again.

Next to the sorter on the line, *Jan Łaski*'s Canadian fishery observer, a woman, is throwing hake into a basket. She has already lost count twice because she is also watching for pollock in the piles of fish moving past her. As well, she is thinking about starting her letters later today. The letters she writes on the ship are full of detail and contrast: sunrise set alongside a glassful of coffee grounds; the crucifix in the crew's mess room mixed with the moonshine wine the fishermen make from blackcurrant juice; the bo's'n's jokes and the tragic face of the youngest motorman. Fishing areas 5-1a, 5-1b, and 5-2, which contain both La Pérouse Bank's peaks and shadows forty fathoms below the surface, and the Carmanah Point line, 241 degrees true, shooting seaward to deep water. The captain in a rage, or steadfast, or drunk. She thinks the woman in the letters from sea is easier to take – braver, brighter – than the muted, shore-side version of herself.

She counts 150 hake into three baskets so she can test the conversion rate for the Baader 182 filleting machine, then decides to describe the conversion test comedy in her first letter: how she trots along beside the conveyor belt before the test can begin, searching for hake still caught on the production line; how she signals to the sorter to dump her 150 fish onto the belt while she squeezes herself around the heading machine, past the barrier shielding the man working with the filleting blades, to watch the limp, white fillets fall onto the moving grid that carries them through the washer before they drop down to the packing table. How some fillets stick in the machinery, arriving late and ragged at the table, causing the factory foreman to argue that these frayed pieces are not "normal" production. How the men packing the tray sometimes mix the test fillets with other fish, and how she shrieks with rage or laughter when this happens.

She will say in the letter that the men in the factory are good to her most of the time. They are not forced to endure, and at last encompass her, as are the fishermen she works with for hours each day on the trawl deck. The factory workers are patient with her sampling and sorting and counting, pleased, she supposes, with anything other than the sameness of their work.

In the engine room below the crew's quarters, the youngest motorman is using a clean rag to wipe sweat from his face before he drinks water that will taste of the tin cup. He plans to double-check the boiler gauges immediately, not because there is any trouble, but to keep himself from thinking. It is fourteen days since *Jan Łaski* off-loaded her cargo of frozen fish to the mother ship in American waters. The fishing ship, in return, took on board: parts for the auxiliary engine; thousands of cardboard cartons for packing frozen hake blocks (two-thirds of these are for other Polish ships on the grounds); several tons of food – meat, potatoes, rice, cabbage, and cooking oil – as well as items purchased by the crew – vodka, beer, cigarettes, and chocolate – and the mail. For the motorman, there was a letter from his mother, who prays the Pacific Ocean will not rise up in fury to take him from her.

The motorman thinks it will not be a Pacific storm that pushes him out of the engine room's straight-edged security into the slippery green salt water. He wonders if he invented the girl he thought he married at the Church of Our Lady in Gdańsk, ten days before this voyage began. He has received no letters from her to prove she exists.

She has run away to Warsaw, is living in the Victoria Inter-Continental Hotel with a man who wears a beautiful grey wool suit. She has confessed to the priest about what happened the first night of their marriage. Now, she lives in the convent, repentant. She is sleeping with his best friend, a bricklayer who never sets foot in the dangerous world outside of Poland. She has burned to death in a fire, been crushed in a train accident. Her mother, and his, will not send him a telegram with bad news while he is at sea. The disastrous words are waiting for him on shore. The Baader mechanic has told him of similar happenings. The motorman wipes his forehead again. He sees the chief engineer watching him from his glass-partitioned office in the centre of the engine room.

The chief engineer, mindful of the boy lost overboard in these waters from *Jan Łaski*'s sister ship last season, one of the helmsmen, he thinks it was, is keeping an eye on his youngest motorman. At the same time, he is reviewing bridge hands in preparation for tonight's game.

Afternoon

The bo's'n is the only fisherman on the trawl deck. The net is out, its thick wires disappear down the ramp into the water, tracked by the churning, white line of the ship's wake. The fog has thinned over a low, grey swell. The last haul, just after dinner at noon, was only five tons of hake mixed with tough-skinned dogfish and a few yellowtail rockfish, pushing the factory into production for less than two hours.

The bo's'n looks into the drying room where boots are set in careful pairs with blue-checked shirts and padded jackets lining the exhaust pipes above them. In the cabin he shares with the second bo's'n, their belongings, from nail clippers to their wives' photographs, are arranged separately in the desk drawers, on the shelves of the one tin locker, and on the hooks fastened to the bulkheads. It is understood that this precise division of goods is necessary to demonstrate that a man may not assume he knows his neighbour entirely, even when he lives and works within a hand's reach of him.

The bo's'n reaches up to touch a smaller jacket hanging on the pipe. The woman. *Jan Łaski* has to carry a Canadian observer in these waters, of course, but why would a woman come to sea with fishermen? It is not natural. But here she is, jammed in with them on the starboard side bench, waiting to haul; running in a shuffle down the slippery, tilted deck as they do; standing at the stern as the huge codend crawls up the ramp; pitching stinking dogfish over the side; wading through mountains of soft hake. She takes their help with her fish basket and her broken weigh scales and her dull knives. When they work through the night, she gives them her white face and her weariness, which are the same as their own. On the ship, she becomes part of the fishermen, and because of this, she is divided from all other women. Unnatural. The bo's'n brushes hake scales from her jacket sleeves, then turns out the pockets so they will dry faster.

He hears a small, repeated sound over the mutter of the main engines, and steps back onto the deck. She is kneeling in the covered area, amidships, taking hake from a basket, measuring them against a marked board, then tossing them into another basket. A tightly bound black scarf hides her hair, broadens her face and hardens its features, obliterating the woman the bo's'n knows. He is suddenly furious, wishing he could shake this strange, fierce female creature until she softens and remembers she is only a woman. She looks up at him, unsmiling, until he walks away.

Evening

Jan Łaski moves along a line of pinnacles 400 fathoms below her keel, the trawl net trailing at mid-water depth. The captain is in his cabin, performing the rituals that will enable him to bear his weariness beyond his closed door, up the ladder to the bridge: the splash of cold water, four sips of whisky, the bunk remade.

The radio officer is still in the radio room, although there are no tasks for him to perform there. He is listening to transmissions from the Polish ships working in the Bering Sea, twelve days north. The voices on these ships are complaining to one another about their upcoming crew change in Seward, Alaska, a port too small to permit anyone to avoid the sight of other crew members, or even to shop successfully. The radio officer already knows what Seward looks like, and he has no friends on Bering Sea ships this season, yet he continues to listen to the weary men far to the north, who now begin to repeat their mild complaints.

The man who sorts the fish and the others from the factory crew are sleeping. The passageways leading to their dark cabins are lined with the green hills and narrow Polish streets of their dreams.

The woman is sitting on her bunk in the dark, listening to the sea rush past below the porthole. *Morze*. The sea. A neuter noun. *Statek*. The ship. A masculine noun. Jan Łaski, 1455 to 1531. Scholar, diplomat. Crown chancellor of Poland. Journeyed by sea to the Holy Land and the Arab countries in 1500. Thereafter worked to ensure Poland would always have her Baltic ports. She wonders if Jan Łaski came to love the ship that carried him to the Holy Land and what the sailors thought of him.

In a while, she puts on the light and takes a white, blue-rimmed water pitcher from its lashing on the shelf underneath the porthole. She fills the pitcher from the trickle of warm water at the sink and begins to wash her hair, sorting through its wind-snarled knots as quickly as the fishermen on deck untangle the trawl web, filling the white jug again and again until the water pouring over her head runs clear.

The motorman sits in the chief engineer's cabin, watching him play bridge with the doctor, the *technolog*, and the factory foreman. Now and then, he looks into the darkness behind the wandering Jew plant which trails across the engineer's closed porthole, satisfied that the talk and laughter of the card players have submerged the sound of the sea. The motorman has already spooned black tea into five glasses, set out the sugar, and sliced a lemon. He waits now for the water to boil.

The bo's'n is alone on the fishermen's bench behind the winch, splicing polypropylene lines.

Night

Close to midnight, the ship is quiet. The fog has dissolved on a rising southeast wind. The radio officer has gone to his cabin at last. The bridge players and the motorman sleep deeply while *Jan Łaski* sways on a wider swell. The bo's'n gently closes his cabin door.

On the bridge, the captain stands by a window open to the blowing darkness. He has given orders for the first officer to set the trawl again when he comes on watch at midnight. The wind will shift the hake schools, and the dawn haul may be worthwhile. The woman is watching the sea gather force from a chair bolted down beside the centre window overlooking the bow. The captain murmurs her name when he says good night and goes below.

When the captain lies down in his bunk, for an instant he sees a boy in a bed beside a window on a summer night fifty years ago, in a village across the world. Stars shine through the soft dark, a breeze flows over the rye fields, the earth seems to roll gently towards him, carrying him into sleep.

Jan Łaski is riding heavy seas when the woman leaves the bridge. The boat deck doors are latched against the waves, the passageways and stairwells are empty. There is only the ship climbing hills of dark water, pouring herself down ocean slopes and climbing again. Standing on the soaked trawl deck, the woman feels the flow of her breath lengthen to follow the repeated, gathering rush and fall of the sea, and wonders if it is the same for *Jan Łaski*'s sailors and fishermen, asleep behind their closed cabin doors.

Before she gets into her bunk, she discovers the bo's'n has kept his month-old promise and made her a cord of foursquare knots. He has lashed a length of precisely ridged knotwork to the grommets on her duffel bag, making a handle so well fastened, so like the bag's bleached white canvas in colour, that it might always have been there.

AFTER THE WAR

War's long afterward is a daily presence on the Polish and Russian ships working in our waters. Ordinary words and acts contain memories.

Two, three, four spoonfuls of sugar are stirred into the black tea drunk on the bridge and behind the winch on the trawl deck. Sugar is sweet comfort and four spoons of it now make up for times when there was none. Alexei Gregorievich, *Mys Osipova*'s trawl master, says when he was a boy, his grandmother kept an empty sugar bag on her kitchen shelf to remind her grandchildren that sugar used to be, and might one day come again.

Mothers and grandmothers are mentioned often on the ships. Mothers in St Petersburg and Petropavlovsk who, for years, hid forbidden images of St Michael the Archangel behind photographs of impossibly young, long-dead soldiers, still in need of an angel's care.

Mothers who cleared rubble from the streets of Warsaw and Gdańsk in 1945 and will not leave these cities now, no matter where their children want them to be. Mothers and grandmothers who still dig potatoes and pick wild berries every winter.

Most of the fathers and grandfathers of the men on the ships were at the battles for Stalingrad or Warsaw or Berlin. They were wounded and never fully recovered, or they were killed. "A wide road leads to war," the Russians say, "but there is only a narrow path home again."

On *Mys Osipova*, the captain sits at his desk with Lenin's portrait above him, watching videos the Canadian boats send over to us in watertight bags tied to the codend. While I work at the table with *Mys Osipova*'s fishing and factory production logs spread out beside me, the Russian captain and commissar marvel at movies showing dolls who come alive to kill their owners or rogue policemen whose pistols never run out of bullets. Late one morning, the gunfire and screaming stop and I look up from my papers to see a Russian video on the screen.

The film is gritty black-and-white, shot too fast. No sound track accompanies the bundled figures stumbling oddly, quickly in the snowy streets. The figures are all women and children or old men. Sometimes they halt and lean against black buildings. Some of them fall over bodies hidden under the snow. The film ends suddenly, freezing forever the people caught in the Battle of Stalingrad.

Beyond the captain's window, Estevan Point is a blurred blue ridge. *Mys Osipova* is rocking gently on a calm sea. But the captain and I are both leaning forward, our hands outstretched as if to reach into the TV screen and pluck out the cold, wild-eyed creatures we have been watching so we can hold them cupped in our palms, close to our mouths, and warm them with our breath. When I look at the captain, I wonder if my face, like his, has gone empty and pale.

Sometimes a few unexpected words bring back the war. *Rekin*'s captain, the chief engineer, and I are waiting for our lifeboat to bring the Canadian captains on board for their yearly visit. The Poles are laughing over a story I told them about my son when he was three or four years old, making shoe-box beds for frogs upstairs in the house on Quadra Island. "What's the first thing you remember from when you were a boy, Captain?" I ask, and there is a small silence.

"Fire," the captain whispers at last. He clears his throat. "Fire and noise." He raises his hand and lets it drop, fluttering his fingers to show the bombs falling. "I am running in the forest with my mother. We never went back to home."

Four years ago, on my first Polish ship, Captain Wrona spread a map over our charts and showed me the Katyn Forest. Here, in 1940, the Russians executed thousands of Polish officers, buried them in a mass grave, then blamed the Nazis when the bodies were found.

Now, the Poles and Russians fish within sight of each other off our coast, but when Tofino Traffic calls

Aquarius or another Polish ship and asks them to take a radio message for the Russians, the answer will come back, "I am sorry, sir, but we have no contact with these vessels."

This year, for the first time, the Russians also remember Katyn Forest. On *Mys Obrucheva*'s trawl deck one morning in early September, Boris is sitting in his bo's'n's chair, reading aloud from a copy of the news clips signalled to the ship from Moscow. Kolya and Sasha lean on the winch beside him, listening to an account of the government's admission of responsibility for the Katyn massacre.

When Boris finishes reading, he gets up and motions for me to sit. The four of us stare down the length of *Mys Obrucheva*'s trawl deck, beyond the stern ramp and out to sea. Two or three cables off our port quarter, the Polish ship *Orlen* is passing us. "They know about Katyn?" Sasha asks. I nod. "And you knew?"

"Yes."

After a moment, Boris points at the *Orlen*, then draws a circle in the air and points back at himself, Sasha, and Kolya. Do they ask you about us? he means. I nod again and the three men look at me expectantly.

Sasha translates one word at a time while I struggle between Russian and English. "I say to the Poles that many on the Russian ships are '*normal'nyi*,' ordinary and good, as they are themselves." When I leave to go down to the factory, Boris, Kolya, and Sasha are bent over the paper again, reading the fifty-year-old news of Katyn.

All of the foreign ships must carry a Canadian pilot between Constance Bank off Victoria and Vancouver harbour. The captain will order coffee; the pilot will thank him, and after this, if there is no course change and the water is calm, the silence on the bridge can stretch for miles.

We were in this silence on a Polish ship one night in Active Pass until I asked our pilot when he first went to sea. He was nineteen, he said, in the merchant marine on a freighter out of Montreal at the end of 1945. They were bound for Gdańsk with a cargo of food, machine parts, and wild horses from Alberta. The Canadian ship manoeuvred around a sunken German hull in Gdańsk harbour and the Alberta horses were corralled near the docks in the ruined city. They were to be railed into the Soviet Union to replace the farm machinery destroyed in the war.

Our captain stepped forward to stand at the bridge window beside the pilot and me. He was only a small boy then, he said, in Gdańsk with his mother, but he remembered the horses from Canada. He remembered how wild and frightened they were.

Forty-five years later, *Antares*'s captain flinches a little when the jets fly above us at the end of the Remembrance Day ceremony at Victory Square in Vancouver. Beside him, I am remembering that only the accidental grace of being born in Canada has made me ignorant of war. Bombs have fallen and fires have flared in the night, children have run into the forest, always in another country.

DELFIN

I was afraid of the first officer on the *Delfin*. He worked the night watch for twelve hours, 2000 to 0800, with the second officer, whom the captain had assigned to keep the fishing logs. The second officer's mistakes were abundant at first. He and I laboured over log entries for species codes, for the ship's position, for the time when our trawl had been shot to the sea, the depth at which we had dragged the gear and the minute when the heavy steel trawl doors had clanged back up the ramp, as well as over entries for the names and CFV numbers of the Canadian draggers who delivered fish to us on joint venture.

The first officer ignored us. He paced the confines of the bridge, carrying the parallel rulers from the chart room in his right hand, tapping them on the window ledge, on the radar hood, and the tea stand, smacking them down sharply enough, now and then, to make the second officer and me jump back from the logbook, startled.

When the paperwork was finished at last, usually between 2200 and 2300, I would bundle my notes into the black ring binder that enclosed the observer's report on the ship. The second officer would nod to me, thankful that our enforced time together was over for another night. I might stand for a moment or two then, watching the sounder screen over the first officer's shoulder, but he would neither move nor speak, so I would leave the bridge and go down to the factory for the last time before I went to my cabin to sleep.

One night the first officer turned aside from the sounder to point at my copy of *The Brothers Karamazov* lying beside the VHF radio. "Perhaps Canada is not entirely a barbaric nation after all," he said.

"Perhaps not," I replied. After this, we progressed, a sentence or two each evening when the logbooks were done, through the strength and glory of medieval Poland; beyond the Polish army's triumph over the Teutonic Knights at the Battle of Grunwald to King Jan Sobieski's seventeenth-century rescue of Vienna, besieged by the Turks at her gates. Then, the 300-year-long darkness, over which we leapt to arrive at the radiance of Pope John Paul II.

I listened while the first officer talked. He seemed to be satisfied with me, and I glowed in the light of his approval. In the factory, the men automatically approved of me, all I had to do was be there with them, wearing

Chanel No. 5 perfume if possible, but if not, no matter. On the trawl deck, I had to demonstrate a little more depth, but not much. A sense of humour. Some willingness to work. Enough intelligence to keep out of the way of lines and booms and hurrying fishermen. But to cause the first officer to admit that I was not a barbarian, to stop his parallel rulers from slamming down with the force of an axe blow, I had to know that the Second World War began at Westerplatte, outside Gdańsk harbour, and that it was really Józef Konrad Korzeniowski who wrote *Lord Jim* and *Heart of Darkness*, not an Englishman called Joseph Conrad.

After nearly two weeks on the ship, I was reading, close to midnight, in the pool of yellow light pouring from the swing lamp above the chart table while I waited for the second officer. The first officer came to stand beside me. I slumped into the table, my body softened by tiredness and the lateness of the hour, by the warmth of his expression.

Gently he took the book from my hands and read aloud, "At Hanukkah time the road from the village to the town is usually covered with snow, but this year the winter had been a mild one." He closed the book and placed it beside my folded hands on the La Pérouse Bank chart. "Isaac Bashevis Singer," he said, adding almost absent-mindedly, "a Jew."

The book's pages fluttered through my fingers. "Zlateh the Goat." "When Shlemiel Went to Warsaw." "The Elders of Chelm and Genendel's Key." "Menaseh's Dream." "Rabbi Leib and the Witch Cunegunde."

"Children's stories," I whispered, desperate to win back my status as a non-barbarian. "Stories from Poland. I wanted to know...."

The first officer interrupted. "All you need to know is that Poland is a clean country now. Cleansed of the Jews." He had turned aside, showing me the line of his profile, sharp and pale. I stepped back from him. The arctic white peaks and shadowed crevasses of a clean country sprang up between us. In the frozen silence, my rubber boots squeaked foolishly against the doorsill. One more step and I would be beyond the chart room on my way to the stairs leading down from the bridge. "What could you know about this in Canada?" the first officer asked me. "You have so many things, and little experience in these matters."

In the chart-room doorway, I remembered another Canada, another place of many goods and supposed riches, which is why it was called Canada. I know a woman whose mother was made to work there. Her job was finding the wedding rings and coins sewn into jacket seams, or hidden inside the dolls and toy bears piled in the warehouse called Canada at Auschwitz.

I looked back over my shoulder at the first officer. Words flew from my mouth like stones. "You disgrace yourself. And the Catholic Church. And Poland." I picked up the black ring binder and the Isaac Bashevis Singer stories and left the bridge.

I heard nothing from the first officer until after dark the next day. The deck crew were winching on board our last codend from *Capt. J. Fiddler* when the intercom spat out an order from the bridge, and the trawl bo's'n, who never looked directly at the first officer or said his name, took my arm and pointed up top. I was afraid, but I climbed the ladder to the boat deck and the bridge. The first officer, his mouth twisted with contempt, was listening to the VHF transmit a slow, quiet voice. The man who runs the *Capt. J. Fiddler* has a slight speech impediment which blurs some of his words. He was asking if the *Delfin* wished to return the empty codend immediately, or wait until first light. The VHF microphone clattered down on the instrument console. "Is this a child speaking, or a defective?" the first officer demanded.

I looked past him into the night. "Do you want to return the net now, or in the morning?" I asked. He turned his back, shrugged, waved towards the deck. I picked up the microphone and told the *Capt. J. Fiddler* we would put the codend to the sea now.

It was dark as I left the bridge, and when I reached the stern ramp, the empty codend was already sliding down the steel slope into the sea. *Delfin* steamed full ahead, leaving the *Capt. J. Fiddler* far astern, searching the black water without the help of our deck lights.

Later, I saw that twenty-two tons of hake and 400 kilograms of dogfish had been entered in the fishing log as a delivery from the "*Kapt. Fiedler,*" a boat undoubtedly owned and run by Jews, the first officer said. After I had cut out the logbook page with my pocket knife and ordered it rewritten with the correct boat name, I went to my cabin, leaving the day's paperwork to be done tomorrow.

For the rest of the voyage, the second officer delayed the logbook entries a little longer each night, so I worked later and later. The first officer spoke only in Polish on the bridge, sometimes slamming down the parallel rulers again. He did not bother to hide his search through my black binder, smearing and crumpling its pages. The bo's'n continued not to look at the first officer, even when he came down onto the trawl deck to give orders. We no longer received codends from the *Capt. J. Fiddler,* which had gone into Ucluelet for a day or two, then fished for other Polish ships.

When the *Delfin* steamed beneath Lions Gate Bridge entering Vancouver harbour, I was on my hands and knees washing the floor of my cabin. I was convinced that if I scrubbed hard enough, I could wash away my certainty that the department of fisheries, the Canadian fishermen, and anyone else the Poles might complain to in Vancouver, would blame me for making trouble – for my book of children's stories by Isaac Bashevis Singer, for my friend's mother who had worked in the other Canada, and, most of all, for my fear of the first officer.

A year later, someone on another Polish ship handed me a parcel from *Delfin's* trawl bo's'n. He would be retired now, I remembered, in Katowice, hundreds of kilometres inland. The crumpled paper contained a string of rough-cut Baltic amber. "*Bursztyn,*" the Poles call it. I lifted the necklace up to the light, pleased with its honey-coloured translucence, then fastened it around my neck and felt the amber's protective warmth, as I knew the bo's'n intended I should.

EUCHARIST

The bread dough lives in a lidded oak trough across from the ovens. On a shelf above the trough are long wooden rolling pins and a brush for painting the tops of the loaves with water. Below are brass balance scales. *Maszyna sercem statku*, the chief engineer says. The engine is the heart of the ship. No, says the baker, the heart of the Polish ship *Mors* is here, in the bread.

Twice a week he scoops a portion of the dough into a tin bucket, setting it aside to be put back into the trough, along with more flour and water, when the morning's bread baking is done. He adds one part rye flour and two parts white from the bins beside him to the remaining sourdough, then a handful of salt and some warm water before he kneads the mixture with broad sweeps of his arms. Thirty-seven times he pinches off a piece of dough the size of his two fists and shapes the lump into a loaf with one or two thrusts across the floured oak board. When the narrow black bread pans are full, the loaves are slashed three times with a razor blade, brushed with water, and left to rise until they meet the fierce dry heat of the brick-lined ovens.

On Thursdays, the baker makes hundreds of the white rolls we eat at teatime with cheese or sausage or honey. He makes long, thin loaves rolled around sweet apple or poppy-seed filling some Saturdays.

The bread on the ship is good, *Mors*'s chief steward says comfortably, but it is not so fine as it was in the village when I was a boy. From time to time then, the grandmothers baked the leaves of herbs – horseradish or dill – on the bottom of the loaves. And the bread was round, big enough to last for a week.

When the steward says this, I remember the pilot who navigated a Russian grain carrier out of Prince Rupert harbour and received a loaf of bread as a parting gift instead of the whisky or brandy sometimes offered on wealthier ships. Not pleased, he dropped the bread on the deck of the pilot boat and it rolled overboard. I imagine this loaf, a dark, heavy circle, sliding into the sea off Triple Island on the north coast.

The chief steward continues. We have good flour even on the ship, he is saying, Polish flour, not the Russian stuff which must be shaken into – how do you say it? – a sieve to take out the threads from the bag and other pieces. Like this rice. You have seen this broken rice I take on board my ship from Soviet Union?

Yes, I know about the broken rice. The cooks have set it aside, although on the Russian ships working in these waters other years, we ate the rice fragments. But this hake season, the Russians had not enough money to pay for our fish and they are not here.

On *Mors* we have enough bread that I can send some over to our catcher boats if I wish. *Można*, the captain shrugs. You may. It is not my problem.

Four loaves wrapped in heavy plastic go into a bag which the bo's'n ties next to the orange floats on the empty codend *Mors* sends back to the Canadian draggers after every haul. The net and the bread, both buoyed by the floats, will churn in our wake until the smaller Canadian boat retrieves them from the sea.

The bo's'n and I might tie one or two salmon or a lingcod alongside the bag of bread going over to the Canadians. He and I lean on the rusted steel ledge over the stern, watching one codend crammed with hake being hauled close to our ramp while the empty codend we are returning with gifts attached recedes into the distance. No-one ever tells us if the bread and fish reach the Canadian draggers.

Once in a while during the months on joint venture, *Mors* receives a package on the hawser line holding the full codend: coffee for me from *Ocean Selector; Playboy* magazines for the fishermen from *Sharlene K.* Last year, one of the draggers finished catching its portion of the Soviet hake quota and the crew sent the Russian ship *Mys Obrucheva* a present to celebrate: a partly eaten bag of raisins; half a tin of Tang; three envelopes of instant cocoa mix. Boris Nikolaievich, the trawl master, Kolya, and the others had eaten only hake with bread for supper hours earlier, but they did not touch these offerings. I gave in to the raisins.

Unless *Mors* has been supplementary fishing – trawling with our own gear at night when we don't receive enough fish from the Canadian boats – I sit beside the bo's'n on the bench at the edge of the trawl deck in the mornings, waiting for fish from *Sharlene K.* or breakfast, whichever comes first. Breakfast will be milk soup, scrambled eggs, bread and butter and plum jam, tea or cocoa. On *Sharlene K.* and the other draggers, they are eating fried eggs and bacon or sausage or ham along with pancakes or waffles, toast, maybe fried potatoes, even pork and beans. There will be oranges, grapefruit, slices of melon, as well as fruit juice, milk, and coffee.

On the Russian ships, breakfast was black tea, dry biscuits, and a woody yellow conserve made from a fruit whose name no-one knew.

By dinner time at noon, *Mors* is usually ready to receive her second codend of the day from the Canadian fishermen. If we hurry, all of us on deck are thinking, we can haul this fish on board and get it into the tanks before we eat. Tomato-dill soup, chicken with rice and green peppers. We have food like this every day on the Polish ships. Pudding on Sundays.

If I miss breakfast, then dinner, the captain's face will darken with irritation. But on this ship, the shame of being different from the others, of being the fishery observer and female, not Polish, makes an inner emptiness food cannot fill. The acts of eating – biting and tearing, chewing, swallowing – frighten me. It seems safer to starve my hidden hollow place in an attempt to diminish it.

The Russians, too, tried sometimes to hide their shame before strangers. Visitors to the captain's cabin on *Mys Osipova* and *Mys Obrucheva* drank vodka with the Party commissar, who told them his title was "first mate," and that all was well on the ship. At the captain's table, a silent woman served pirogi stuffed with mushrooms or ground meat, along with plates of cucumbers and tomatoes. The captain, the commissar, the chief engineer, and I, too, would eat modestly, casually, as if this food were our daily fare. But the pirogi and fresh vegetables were taken from the ship's small stores for hospitality. When there were no guests, the captain, the commissar, and the rest of us ate rainwater soup or rice pudding for supper.

Mors receives her last codend on the 1991 joint-venture hake fishery from the Canadian dragger *Sunnfjord* on the day Mikhail Gorbachev asks the West for grain, meat, and sugar to prevent famine in his country.

Off-loading frozen fish to the mother ship farther out at sea takes time, but, at last, near to midnight, *Mors* is steaming for Constance Bank anchorage where she will take on a pilot for Active Pass and Vancouver harbour.

The wind scraping the darkened trawl deck tastes like winter. From out here, I can look into the warm light of the ship's kitchen where the sourdough still breathes, waiting for another baker coming from Poland to Vancouver tomorrow or the next day to begin a new voyage on *Mors*. The chief steward is arranging platters of sausage and cheese and bread for the night meal. He motions to the heaps of food in front of him when he sees me watching. *Można*, he says. You may. But I shake my head. I cannot.

On *Mys Obrucheva*, one Russian fisherman spoke the old words for grace sometimes when the deck crew and I crouched on the bench behind the winch late at night, eating fried potatoes. *Chlebwino-granda mir Bóg*, he would say. In this wine and bread lie the peace of God. There was no wine on *Mys Obrucheva* or *Mys Osipova*, and only just enough bread. But there was enough of the peace of God on the worn Soviet ships for me to remember them often when they were not with us this season on the offshore fishing grounds west of Vancouver Island.

More than a stretch of sea and the width of another country separates the Russians from me now. I will eat as I wish this winter. They will not. "The man with a warm coat doesn't know how anyone can feel cold," the fishermen on *Mys Osipova* used to tell me, laughing. "Fear life, not death," they said last year on *Mys Obrucheva*.

KANTAR

The sea is not freedom. But it is in the likeness of freedom. It is the symbol. How beautiful is freedom itself if the mention of it, if its likeness, fills a man with happiness.

—Vasilii Grossman
Forever Flowing

Roman and Czesław worked on the *Kantar*, the smallest, oldest ship in Poland's Pacific fleet, called "Grandfather *Kantar*" by the crew. Roman was the trawl bo's'n, side-long glancing and watchful as a wolf, as suited to secret places on hillsides and in the forest, I thought, as to the trawl deck's open spaces. Roman understood how much I needed him to wink at me, confirming that, yes, we all hate it when the captain comes down on deck to give us orders we don't need. He knew I feared the lengthy observer radio conferences, and often left a glass of tea beside the winch for me to find when I finished in the radio room. One afternoon early in the voyage, he brought his trawl net diagrams into the bright, hot glare of my amidships cabin. While I noted the length of the warp and the width of the net's wings, Roman glanced at the crumpled sheets on my bunk and brushed a hand lightly over my sweat-dampened pillow. After that day, I slept thirty or forty minutes most afternoons in the dim coolness of the bo's'n's cabin, my boots beside me, Roman a few steps beyond the door, asleep on the trawl deck bench.

Czesław was fifty-four years old, so hard and thin his face looked carved from bone. His hair was brown fading to grey, cut in rough, intractable spikes. He wore a knife on his belt and stood straight, fiercely elegant in black boots and work pants. Czesław had sailed thirty-three years on tankers running from Odessa to Marseille; on Greek ships steaming out of Piraeus through the Strait of Hormuz to Basra and Dhahran. He had worked on freighters out of Mediterranean and Black Sea and Indian Ocean ports. He knew the narrow streets, the bars, and the mailboxes nearest the docks in Port Elizabeth, Houston, Corpus Christi, Istanbul, Singapore, and Tripoli. He had a wife and one son. He wished he had spent his life differently.

Czesław and I stood together at *Kantar*'s stern four or five times a day, waiting for the codend on the transfer line to reach our ramp. We sat on the fisher-men's bench drinking tea, or we sprawled on piled nets in the sun, or squatted like children, resting our backs against the bulkhead. Every evening, we leaned on the aluminum ladder by the starboard side of the deck, watching light fade out of the sky while *Arctic Ocean* or *Zeal* or *Capt. J. Fiddler* followed the ship with the last codend for the day. All the while, despite our lurching entrances into the forest of a foreign language, and our silences, Czesław and I knew each other as if we were blood brother and sister.

Often we failed to communicate, pouring out a river of sentences in our own language, ending with a badly pronounced, desperate word or two in the other's speech, staring at each other in pity. Sometimes we managed to fill in the blanks. *Praca*, I would say, work, and hold my hand outstretched, palm flat, *i morze*, the sea. Work and the sea, then my hand would sketch a writing gesture. Work and the sea and writing. Life. Mine.

Czesław nodded. *Nie ma*, he said, tilting his own flattened palm. *Nie ma* balance. No balance. No good.

I tried to provoke his sympathy one day. The ship, *statek*, was difficult, *trudna*, I said, for a not-young woman. I made a downward sweep along my body with both hands, pausing at my head and heart to show that I meant all of me, body, mind, and spirit. Czesław laughed and mimicked the gesture against his own body. Not easy for a not-young man either.

After thirty days on the ship, I slammed my cabin door in a rage because the captain refused to believe that we had drifted south of the Carmanah Point line until the U.S. Coast Guard appeared off our stern. I sulked for a week when I got erratic results from my conversion rate tests on the factory machines and the *technolog* invented an excuse for every variation. Roman and Czesław, who had been at sea nearly five months, contained their weariness within their unfaltering care of the nets, lines, and shackles, the two younger fishermen on the crew, and me. Roman made a white flower from strapping tape and tied its stiff, star-pointed petals and trailing leaves to the handle of my fish basket. Czesław gave me a length of Manila rope and made me learn the overboard knot – left hand holds the rope, right hand brings the other end around the body, across the first loop and up through it, then pulls tight – so that once the rope was fastened to a cleat or lashed around the waist of a man firmly braced on deck, I could, if I must, go into the sea and return.

Day after day as Roman and Czesław and I worked together, out of the current of words and signs and silences running between us, I distilled their central message to me. Don't do as we have done. Don't work at sea forever. Sea is narcotic, Czesław said one day. Roman nodded. And life, the life lived by those on shore, real life, Czesław rolled his hands to simulate an endlessly moving film, this life continues without us.

One night, long after dark, when we were all exhausted, Czesław sat on an upturned wooden box, facing Roman and me on the trawl deck bench. He leaned forward, elbows on his knees, and spoke in Polish to Roman, who looked past him into the dark and said nothing. For me, Czesław held up his spread fingers. Five fingers. Five more years on the ships. And then? He pointed southeast, to where the land was supposed to be if it had not drifted beyond our reach forever. Swiftly, delicately, he mimed digging with a shovel. Not a garden. A grave.

At Burlington Northern dock in Vancouver, Roman and Czesław loaded my bags into a taxi. I climbed in, and pulled them, unresisting, into the back seat to sit beside me. They refused to ask where we were going.

When we arrived at the seaplane dock, I paid the cab driver to wait and drive them back to the *Kantar*. They looked at the Twin Otter with horror and focused instead on the sea beyond the plane dock. When it was time for me to walk down the ramp, Roman put his hand on my shoulder. Try, he said. Czesław held his flattened palm steady. Try for balance. We smiled brilliantly at one another. I looked back from the door of the plane and saw they were still there, arms folded, watching me. I lifted my hand, releasing them. We turned away from each other, and in that motion consigned ourselves to the land.

BROKEN

Dear Cypris, if thou savest those at sea,
I perish wrecked ashore; save also me.

—Greek, 6th c.

John Evans, who started fishing on a trawler out of Grimsby, England, when he was a boy, stepped onto the ladder at the Campbell Avenue dock in Vancouver sometime before midnight, January 12, 1985. He was climbing down to the *Pacific Eagle*. The *Eagle* had been laid up in the river for some months until Leo Barros, John, and the rest of the crew had brought her around to gear up for a northern trip. Leo planned to fish either Cape Scott spit or the Goose Island grounds.

The twelfth rung of the ladder was missing and the thirteenth broke under John's feet. He fell into the black cold beneath the chained, half-sunken bumper log waiting on the water below, and found no way back until he saw his mother, young and bright-faced, leaning down to him. When he stood on the deck of the *Pacific Eagle* again, his hands were ripped and bleeding from the barnacles on the pilings. Pain shone like a halo around his body.

He went into the wheelhouse and called Vancouver Traffic for a long time until he remembered the radio batteries had been sent ashore that afternoon. By dawn, he was on his hands and knees. His back was broken.

This year, at the start of another season of not fishing, John is looking out at Esquimalt harbour where a red-hulled freighter lies at anchor, listing to starboard. Saw another just like her, he says, sounding absent-minded, remembering. We were fishing cod on the *Bombardier* off the Russian coast when she went by, all leaned over like that, a red hull, her decks piled with timber. A Greek ship. The Norwegian pilots wouldn't bring her into inside waters when the weather blew up, so she went on around the north cape. Cape Nord. We went that way ourselves a week or so later when we got a trip of fish. Around that cape.

There was wood on the water for miles. The sea was covered with timber.

AT SEA WITH STRANGERS

At midnight, I am standing by the galley door while *Neekis* jogs offshore. *Neekis* is a Canadian dragger working on the joint-venture hake fishery with the Polish ships, and her crew will be glad to be rid of me so they can sleep for a few hours before dawn.

On *Neekis*'s starboard side, within the circle of light flooding from her deck onto the sea, a wooden-hulled lifeboat marked *Antares* slides in the trough of the swell. The lifeboat's tie-up line smacks on the dragger's deck rail. The men on both boats are shouting above the roar of gas and diesel engines and the pounding hiss of the waves. Across a stretch of dark water lies the lighted bulk of the Polish fishing ship *Antares*. *Neekis*'s position is 48 degrees, 34 minutes north, 125 degrees, 30 minutes west, and, except for *Antares*, there is only the sea around us.

John, who runs the *Neekis*, yells at his deck hand to throw my duffel bags down to the Poles, then he turns to me and nods. John is kind enough, but he is tired. He expects me to smile back at him, step forward without hesitating, and jump down to the lifeboat.

When they see me, crouched, ready, the Polish fishermen shout up an urgent command. Don't jump until their boat climbs on the swell as *Neekis* drops, they mean. Pale, unknown faces rise towards me. I jump into outstretched arms, am thrust down on the thwart, a life jacket in my hands. The Polish fishermen cast off. I wave, although I can no longer see the faces of the Canadians or the outline of the *Neekis* clearly, and we move through the dark to *Antares*. Another voyage is beginning and I am afraid, because I am always the stranger on the ship no matter how many times I go to sea.

Captain Wrona is waiting on *Antares*'s bridge, smiling broadly, and at the moment when he reaches for my hand, I believe he is truly glad to see me. He was my first captain three years ago, so he knows I don't get seasick or drunk or talk on the radio constantly, that I can work without bothering the bo's'n or the fishermen on deck and that I won't knock on his door at 0300 to say we just hauled half a ton of widow rockfish and what is he going to do about it.

Captain Wrona is white-haired, tanned, and slim, not much taller than me. I learned on my first voyage that his favourite English phrase is "not necessary," which means "not appropriate," as well as "not required." On *Antares*, I won't be drinking coffee – and possibly spilling it – in the chart room, nor will I be asking for a pencil sharpener when everyone who goes to sea should be able to sharpen a pencil with a pocket knife. Neither will I be shedding any tears. Not necessary.

The captain calls down to the trawl deck for a man to carry my bags to my cabin. I stumble at the top of the stairs, suddenly weary, knowing the starched cotton sheets are piled on my bunk, waiting to be made up; that my alarm clock and boots are likely at the bottom of my duffel bag; that the fish will be on board early in the morning.

"You are tired," Captain Wrona states, motioning briskly for me to hurry down the stairs. "Hungry. It is not necessary. Teatime is also at night." In the crew's mess room, he fetches sausages from the pot simmering in the kitchen, passes the bread and mustard. Men are eating at the tables around us, but I look only at the food on the thick, white plate in front of me, and at the captain's arm, lifting and lowering beside me as he smokes and drinks tea.

When the meal is over and Captain Wrona has gone, I cross the trawl deck to the cabin where my bags lie beside a tin locker jammed next to the life-belt box on the bulkhead. The steward has wrestled the mattress out of the white metal rails enclosing my bunk and put on the bottom sheet. Only the blanket cover and pillow-case are left for me to arrange. I shake the blanket into its white cotton cover, fastening it with the buttons from the tin locker's top shelf, then tie the pillow into its case.

When I lie down, my bed at home and the narrow grey road to the dock in Ucluelet and *Neekis*'s wheelhouse surge onto the screen behind my closed eyes, then sink, forgotten, in a black sea. If I sit up, leaning forward to peer around the corner, a thread of light from the deck will show beneath my cabin door. Otherwise, the darkness in here and beyond the porthole is complete.

In the morning, I reach for my jacket and wrench open the cabin door as soon as I hear the captain's voice on the intercom. *"Bosman,"* he is calling, while a thin, fair-haired man I saw for a moment on the boat deck last night is standing by the speaker outside the mess room, listening. *"Wybieramy za dwadzieścia minut."* Bo's'n, we are hauling back in twenty minutes.

The bo's'n and his crew are turned away from me, talking and laughing. I am afraid of them. The sky is grey and the wind is picking up. No matter how slimed or wet or slanted the trawl deck might have been on other ships, I have never fallen. Today, I will surely fall. I don't know where this bo's'n wants me to stand when we haul fish. I don't know how quickly he and his crew open the huge codends, or if I can get a good view of the fish before they are dumped into the tanks below decks. I don't even know which door leads from the deck down to the factory.

A touch on my arm makes me jump, but the man beside me has a broad, calm face, and he is offering me a glass of coffee topped with a saucer enclosing the steam. By the time I have drunk half the coffee, I know that the man who made it for me is Andrzej, that the

thin man is the bo's'n, Franek, and that I probably will
not fall on the trawl deck today.

Three weeks into the *Antares* voyage, Franek and
Andrzej are standing across from me on the starboard
side of the stern ramp, watching rain fall on a darkening sea. They have already let the transfer line off the
stern winch to trail in our wake while *Pacific Charmer*
passes the ship's port quarter and turns into the wind to
follow us. When Franek hears the Canadian boat whistle, he will signal the bridge to begin hauling with our
main winches.

The mesh in the codend might or might not be
ripped. There may be too much fish for our tanks, or
not enough. The hake may be soft from being held in
the trawl too long, or firm and easy to fillet. Neither
Franek nor the deck crew nor Captain Wrona nor
Krys, the first officer, nor I will be surprised by any of
these things. The crew on the *Pacific Charmer* might
wave, or they might ignore us. We will not be surprised by this either. The fishermen on *Pacific
Charmer* are in Canada, while Franek and I and the
others are in Poland even though we can see Vancouver Island some days. The only home and work and
friends available to us are on *Antares*. Our world has
grown small.

Once the last haul is on board close to midnight,
Franek, Andrzej, and I crowd into my cabin, cramped
together along the iron rail around my bunk, the sleeves
of our yellow rain jackets crackling against each other.

Franek guards the steaming kettle on my desk as it lurches against its lashing, following the steepening roll of the ship. Andrzej is opening the old cocoa tin which holds coffee ground to fine powder. I am hunched back into the hood of my jacket trying to get warm, shifting on the rail while I search for a place to prop my feet, balancing my field notebook and the calculator on my soaked, denim-covered knee.

In my Rite in the Rain All Weather line-ruled notebook, I write: "Haul #352, 2240, August 19, 1989, *Pacific Charmer*: Codend height 1.4 metres. Length 10.2 metres." (Calculate volume of symmetrical codends by multiplying the radius squared by pi, times the length. Multiply this total by .9 for the density.) Theoretically then, the codend held fourteen metric tons, plus 120 kilograms. Surely ninety per cent of the mass of fish was hake. Five per cent pollock? I never know for certain until I count how many pollock in every hundred fish along the line in the factory. And the dogfish layered all through the codend? Maybe 300 kilograms. Wait. Dogfish are lighter than they look. Intransigent, too, with their sandpaper skin and darning-needle spines jamming in portholes and scuppers. The yellowtail and red snappers on the deck-estimate list will have to be included in the pollock percentage. I smear pencilled stars beside these notes and shift the book to my other knee.

If Franek and Andrzej see this codend estimate calculated from a biologist's formula, they will roll on the deck laughing. The Polish fishermen know that *Pacific Charmer*'s codend was choke-strapped on the twelfth strengthening band to hold about eighteen tons of hake, and who cares about the pitiful amounts of pollock or dogfish or yellowtail or snapper except me? I feel sorry for myself. My hands are cold. My hair is dirty and wet, dripping down my neck. We had liver for supper. I still have to run the conversion tests on the Baader 188 and 190 production lines, as well as check the deck estimate for *Pacific Charmer*'s haul in the tanks and on the lines in the factory.

Andrzej reaches over to remove the Rite in the Rain notebook and the calculator, tucking them inside the binder labelled TRIP REPORT ANTARES.

"*Tak*. Yes." I gladly let the notebook go and Andrzej pours boiling water over coffee heaped in three glasses anchored on a dampened rag so they won't slide on the table as *Antares* pitches to port, hesitates, then heaves herself upright and slides down to starboard.

"Coffee," Andrzej pronounces gravely, drawing out the first syllable to a drawling North American caw-fee.

"Please. *Proszę*," then, after a deep breath, "*karmazyn, rekin, mintaj, śledź, gdzie dziękuję, mostek,* Katyn Forest, Tadeusz Konwicki, *worek, słownik,* Jaruzelski, stop *maszyna!* Solidarność, *przetwórnia, herbata, kawa, tak, nie ma, dlaczego lewa burta, prawa burta,* Czesław Miłosz – *Unattainable Earth.*"

Andrzej responds to this recital with a vocabulary of his own: "Joint venture, observer, sea, Joanna, Kraków very old city, vodka, *Szkocka* whisky, FBI, CBC, Indians, good, Street Hastings, Liverpool, *Pacific Charmer*, flower, honey, hauling back."

All three of us are smiling now, pleased with ourselves for not sinking into gloom in the rain and dark. Franek offers me a new Polish word, "*śnić*." "Dream," Andrzej translates. "I dream to finish work." A snake of cold air from the porthole lifts our cigarette smoke, loops itself around our bodies, making even Franek shiver. We are not finished work, Franek, Andrzej, and I, nor is anyone else on *Antares*. We are finished only the joint venture, and now we begin on the Polish national hake quota with our own trawl gear. From this night on, we will shoot the net, tow and haul twenty-four hours a day in offshore fishing areas 5-1b or 5-2.

Some hidden change – a slight alteration in our course or in the beat of the engines, the wind a degree or two towards a new direction, some sound too diffused to identify – causes us to shift restlessly, to set down our coffee glasses, tug at our jacket fastenings, knowing it is time to move. Andrzej and Franek and two or three other men are going to dump the last third of *Pacific Charmer*'s codend now that there is more room for fish in the tanks. I am going to the factory with my notebook.

When I step up on the grid beside Bogdan, who sorts the fish as they stream from the tanks, he is throwing dogfish over his shoulder, creating a knee-high pile behind himself. "*Rekin*," he mumbles, "*dużo rekina*." Many dogfish. In the discard pile, limp grey-black backs are collapsed over white bellies. Lumpy flesh bags in loose, rough skin. Turquoise eyes stud the heads.

Once, on another ship, I left the sorter pitching nearly a ton of dogfish out the porthole to go up on deck and watch another haul with still more dogfish larded throughout the hake. When I returned to the factory, I found a tray of sea water by the scupper with dogfish four or five centimetres long swimming about while the stinking bodies of their adult counterparts sailed through the air above them. Dogfish give birth to live young after a gestation period longer than an elephant's, and the sorter had seen a belly moving in one of the dead fish, so he performed a Caesarean. We poured the babies into the sea once they had gained strength.

When I stoop to bundle dogfish, tails together, and begin shoving them out the nearest porthole, Bogdan looks reproachful. Joanna, *nie*, he murmurs. I nod and keep on gathering dogfish. He knows I'll discard them out the porthole or the scupper for ten or twelve minutes, not much more, then begin my own work. Bogdan and I perform this same dance every shift.

The factory is always the same. The light changes little from midday to midnight. Machines scream. Rivers of fish slide along conveyor belts. Our booted feet are either sweating or cold. Our hands in black rubber gloves are white and puffy, stinking of fish, punctured by rockfish and dogfish spines. Hake scales crust the fronts of our jackets, our cheeks, and strands of our hair. Four hours into every shift, Bogdan will begin to arch his back whenever there is a pause in the flow of hake. Every time I bend over the line to count 150 fish for the conversion test, my back will pinch in the same place, below my waist on the right side. My elbow joints feel as if they are shrieking now, when I lift my end of the fifty-kilogram baskets of hake. My mouth twists up on the left side with every basket.

I stand beside Bogdan on the line, counting fish by hundreds: ninety-six hake, three pollock, one snapper; ninety-eight hake, two pollock; eighty-six hake, four pollock, ten dogfish, most of them large. Life is brutal and full of *zasadzkas* – traps. Say this with a smile. Bend. Lift. Stagger. Catch your boot on the floor grating. Lurch into the side of the slime-covered tanks. Breathe while the ship rolls. Take out your notebook. Three per cent pollock? As long as some number within reaching distance of this estimate is in the ship's fishing logs.

To get out of the factory, I have to move past the rack freezers, under the tray-release machine, through the gang of grinning bandits packing fillets into trays, across the lower-deck passageway to the trawl-deck ladder and my cabin. No. We are shooting the net again and the trawl wires are tight at neck level. Back down the ladder, along the lower-deck passageway, up the starboard side of the deck and into the cabin.

Remove rubber apron. Wash hands. Take off jacket covered with hake scales. Grab clipboard and calculator. Climb up two decks, holding onto the handrail on the stairs. Open the door marked "*Mostek*." The bridge.

Krys, *Antares*'s first officer, is on the bridge watch with the second officer from 1600 to 2000, and from midnight to 0800. Tonight, he is crouched over the sounder, searching its screen for hake schools. I touch his shoulder on my way to the fishing logs in the chart room.

Every second or third night, Krys and I drink coffee in his cabin before he goes on watch at midnight. We talk about history and books and movies, and about going crazy at sea. He would go mad in a month, he says, if he didn't put aside almost all thoughts of his family and narrow his focus to the country bordered by *Antares*'s deck rails.

I never yearn for home when I am at sea, but the land sometimes reaches out for me, insisting that I remember Meziadin Junction with the hot dust of summer hanging in the air – I go north from there to Cassiar and Telegraph Creek; west to Stewart on Portland Canal; east to the confluence of the Nass and Meziadin Rivers. Or Hastings Street in Vancouver, that block before Commercial Drive where there is suddenly space and sky and light, as if you were driving by a vacant lot in a small town. Fort St James, outside the old Hudson's Bay store, keys locked inside the car until a boy with thin fingers and a coat hanger gets the door open.

These sensations – the smell of dust on the Meziadin road, the slurred sound of cars on Hastings Street, the smooth, varnished wood on the door into the bar in Fort St James – are still present when I return to myself on the ship and hear the shriek of the Baader machines, or stumble over the trawl wires on deck. I wonder, now and then, if the motormen down in *Antares*'s engine room are walking trails in the Tatra Mountains, if the cook is fifteen again, lounging uneasily by the Kraków Gate in Lublin, waiting for a girl.

Krys says Captain Wrona has already sent one crazy man home on the mother ship. I must look scared because he tells me that he, too, wanders in memories of other places and times, and the only necessity is to recall the trick of returning quickly to the ship when need be. Krys is a kind man. Captain Wrona says he sleeps easily when Krys is on the bridge, but I take this for granted. It is more important to me that Krys is kind. When I finish checking the log entries at 0300, he is still staring at the sounder screen, eating lifeboat ration biscuits from the tin he said he was opening for me. He will order our trawl hauled back at dawn, he says.

Fifteen minutes later, Andrzej and I are sitting on my bunk, legs stretched over the iron side rails because we are wearing our boots. We are staring into the still-black sky beyond my porthole, listening to k.d. lang on an old Soviet tape recorder borrowed from the factory foreman. k.d. lang is singing about watching someone leave and how if she hadn't cheated and lied, she'd be walking by their side. Andrzej and I want to hear "Busy Being Blue," the song that best accompanies waiting to haul in the dead hour before dawn.

"I'd have time on my hands," sings k.d. lang, until she is interrupted by the intercom sputtering, *Bosman, wybieramy*! We are hauling back now. Andrzej is up from the bunk without a word, out the door to the deck.

When I stand, my knees are treacherously weak, but winching the codend on board takes twenty minutes or more, so I can crouch in my doorway, promising my body sleep when this haul is done.

The wind has dropped to fifteen or twenty knots. Fine rain spangles the black planks beneath the deck lights. Almost a thousand metres of trawl wire clicks and whines back onto the drums before the trawl net's web of lines appears. The ropes and meshes on a trawl are arranged in sections called the bosom, belly, wings, and bridle, which means that while I am peering around the edge of my door to see if the codend is showing on the ramp yet, I am wondering if all the trawl fishermen I know – Polish, Russian, and Canadian – imagine their gear is either a winged woman or an angel in harness. Maybe they give their nets names I never hear, names of mothers, wives, sisters, or daughters, of lovers, movie stars, hookers, saints.

Four men trudge past me on their way to the stern, their bodies bowed from the weight of the cable over their shoulders. I turn away, unwilling to look into their eyes. The rain dampening their backs and the resignation in their posture as they kneel, allowing the cable to slide from their shoulders, contains an echo of slave labour that diminishes me, who only watches.

More cable to the stern. Shackle. Haul. Shackle again and haul. My hard hat is set firmly on my head, my hair is tucked in tightly. I am ready to step onto the deck once Franek signals that the codend is in place. There is almost no danger this morning because the net holds only about six tons of fish, maybe less, hake mixed with rockfish, mostly yellowtail and widows. Bogdan and the other men from the factory are standing across the deck from me, looking at the codend with blank faces. There isn't more than an hour or two of work for them here.

While the factory below deck is being fired up, then shut down again almost immediately, the codend will be picked clean, so the gear can be shot to the sea again, towed for hours and hauled, catching not enough fish in a repeated cycle that blurs the boundaries between night and day.

I will no longer know whether I am sleeping at noon or at night. Insistent knocking on the cabin's steel door will wake me. Joanna, *ryba*! Fish. I will push up through layers of sleep as if I were making my way from the ocean floor into the shimmering band of sky light on the sea surface. The brightness will become *Antares*'s deck lights, or the sun leaking around the edge of my jacket hung over the porthole. Wake up and push play for k.d. lang and "Bopalena." "Pine and Stew." "Up to Me." "Tickled Pink." "Hanky Panky." "There You Go." "Hooked on Junk," the song the Poles hate, but I like. "Stop, Look and Listen." "Busy Being Blue." Find boots and net-measuring tape, handle still slimed from last haul. Step onto the deck. Call, irritably, to Franek, moment, *proszę*. Wait. Please.

We live by routine. For the men, twelve hours on, twelve hours off most days. For me, every haul must be checked on deck and in the factory, and its statistics included in daily and weekly catch reports. Length-sex-stomach samples on hake must be performed on the assigned sampling day. All fish to be chosen at random to fill three fish baskets. No grading. No sizing. No counting. Additional samples to be taken if vessel moves more than ten nautical miles. All biological and other quantifiable data to be entered on computer forms with correct codes. The trip report requires descriptions of *Antares*'s procedures for setting, towing, hauling, and transferring codends and trawls; for dumping, processing, packing and freezing fish, and making fish meal. Provide diagrams. Give size and capacity of all machinery. Add times, rates, and temperatures where appropriate.

Every Monday we clean our cabins and the passageways. Every twenty-one days the steward brings clean sheets. Once a month we have fire drill and boat drill. On the bulkhead in my cabin:

> For Canada The Alarm Bells
> 1. Leave out the ship alarm . . . . - -
> Boat #1 life raft #3
> 2. Man overboard . . - -   - - . . rallying point deck
> 3. Water alarm   . . - -   - - . . rallying point deck
> 4. Gas alarm . . - - - - . . rallying point deck
> 5. Fire alarm . . - - rallying point deck

If we abandon ship, my duty in the lifeboat is to row. If we have a collision or some other mishap but are not sinking, my duty is to go to the bridge and help the captain contact the Coast Guard.

We have breakfast at 0730, dinner at 1130, tea at 1530, supper at 1930, tea again at midnight. We eat fish on Friday and a sweet after dinner on Sunday. White rolls on Thursday. Fresh bread twice a week. Almost all of our food is from Poland, brought by the mother ships when we off-load our fish. Every egg bears a tiny red stamp to show it is from Poland. The price of these eggs has more than doubled since *Antares*'s crew left Poland last April. We know this because the ship receives the Warsaw news every day.

Krystov, our radio officer, transcribes Morse code messages to produce the typed newspapers he pins up in the officers' and crew's mess rooms:

August 27, 1989 – On the day following his election as prime minister, Mr. Mazowiecki received the ambassadors of Belgium and the U.S.S.R. as well as a group of bishops from West Germany.

August 29, 1989 – Within the framework of consultations for forming a new government, the prime minister met with the president of the Citizens' Parliamentary Club.

A supermarket in Gdynia has today burned to the ground. Damages are 250-million zlotys.

August 30, 1989 – Today is the anniversary of the country's first agreements with striking Solidarity shipyard workers in August, 1980.

Mail from home provides the details about what is happening in Poland. Letters to the ship go to the maritime agent's office in Anchorage or Vancouver, where they are bundled and sent to sea on the first vessel likely to steam near to our position. The mail is flung over to us in a watertight packet tied to a heaving line, or arrives more sedately in a lifeboat carrying provisions or engine parts as well.

Sea is sea, Captain Wrona says at least once a day with either a laugh or a sigh. And letters are letters. But phone calls home to Poland are in sharper contrast with life on the ship. *Antares*'s radio officer spends the late afternoons switching between transmitters to find either Milli Vanilli singing, "It's a tragedy for me the dream is over," or the Gdynia radio operator, so the people can listen to the lovely voice of their wife, he murmurs.

The wives speak of the same problems over and over, Krystov says. Problems with children, with money, with sickness, with families. What can you do through the telephone line? he asks me while he fiddles with the short-wave frequency, trying to pick up CFUN in Vancouver, or CKDA in Victoria so he can hear the song about broken dreams again. And Krystov's own radio contact with home? "I haven't a phone," he tells me. "Maybe thirty to forty per cent of crew members has a phone at home. I know also the crew members which has a phone but never use it."

The letters and radio phone calls, even the news bulletins, emphasize the distance between ourselves and the others in our lives. Those who stay on land are innocent of the compromises we have made at sea. They don't know how we have subdued ourselves to live in ordinary peace with too-familiar faces and bodies in cramped spaces; how we have levelled our ambitious desires for comfort to accommodate only sometime warmth, occasional cleanliness and laughter, a glass of tea, pudding on Sundays. Krys, the first officer, says, "My wife was on the ship only one time in her life. She came on that ship, look, and ask me, 'How do you live on that box for half a year?' I answer her, 'I don't know.'" The shore dwellers' innocence about the compromises we have made in order to survive sets them and home and land itself apart from us in a distant, perfect dream while *Antares* seems more crowded, grubbier, and ever the same, day after night after day. None of us can escape this sameness as we move slowly in the late summer fog offshore, searching for fish, setting, hauling, and catching little.

We are trawling as long as ten hours now to search for hake before we haul, so the fishermen and I and the factory crew are sleeping more than we are used to, but our vacant-eyed weariness does not diminish. We are tired of each other and of ourselves and of *Antares*. Everyone has sat in the crew's mess on bolted-down chairs at oilcloth-covered plywood tables one too many times; gazed at the map of Vancouver pinned on the bulletin board next to the daily factory-production figure; has drunk tea; reached for the sugar jar or the jam tin in the wooden holders; looked up at the picture of Pope John Paul II blessing us; filled their 220-volt water boilers at the fresh water tank in the corner; butted their cigarettes in bent tin-can ashtrays; played card games with greasy, limp LOT Air cards; and lit one another's cigarettes with old Zippo lighters or thin Polish matches. Everyone has seen the few videos we have on board. Our coffee is nearly gone. There are no more Caro cigarettes in the canteen.

I am locked in my cabin, drawing a diagram of the factory from the sketch in my notebook. My knees are jammed under a plywood table ridged to catch sliding pens and pencils. *Antares* is rolling heavily. Every time we hauled today, the ramp dipped low into the sea, pouring water on deck as far as my cabin door, then rose until it seemed we were hauling out of the sky. The ragged blue curtain on a rusted ring is swinging wildly beside my porthole. The thin twine cord I am making from a chain of codend knots has come loose from its mooring on the iron leg of my bunk. I am wearing red socks, dirty jeans, a black sweater, and a jacket crusted with hake scales. My hands are stiff with salt water and rockfish spine cuts. The Black Madonna of Częstochowa looks down on me from the bulkhead over my bunk. This image of the Mother of God, which rests now in the monastery on Jasna Góra, the Bright Hill, at Częstochowa, was painted by St Luke, legend tells, on a plank from the house of the Holy Family in Nazareth. The icon's known history only sets her further back in Byzantine shadows. She is not like the pink and white, gently smiling Marys of the West. Her face is dark, her eyes hooded, mouth impassive. And her cheek is deeply scarred. The Black Madonna, the playmates on the bulkheads in the crew's quarters, and I are the only women on *Antares*.

When I unlock my cabin door and look out on deck, the fog has lifted and the sea slides and tilts to the edge of a milk-white sky. Below this arc of pure mild light the waves slant every liquid within their reach – the diesel fuel in *Antares*'s tanks, the coffee in our cups, and the blood in our bodies – holding us as we were once held in the small sea that surrounds us before birth. When we sleep on this broad, deep offshore swell, most of us on *Antares* dream.

Captains dream of being alone at the wheel of their ship, straining to keep a course while they steer the careening bulk of the hull along narrow stone streets in Gdańsk and Bydgoszcz, or beside fields seeded with rye and flax.

The sailors dream of hills, mountains even, rising beyond their cabin doors, of mothers kneeling beside their bunks, of the pope dressed as a partisan, carrying a gun and looking sorrowful.

I dream of gardens gone dead, flowers and grass withered and dry. Some nights I step onto a boat that is light in ballast, drifting and rolling on an unnamed river. Other nights, I am the boat and now it is me who is nameless. Sometimes the river narrows, becomes impassable in its upper reaches like Hell's Gate on the Fraser, or I stand beside the Skeena in the north again, smiling, listening to the rush of water until it blurs into the sound of *Antares*'s engines punctured by the ship's alarm bells. Two bells. Only an engine manoeuvre. We are coming alongside *Mazury*, the mother ship, at last.

Once the lines are secure and the huge black rubber bumpers let down to keep the two ships from crashing into each other, off-loading begins. The forward and aft hatches are opened so the cargo slings stuffed with fish-meal sacks and pallet boards stacked with cartons of frozen fish can rise on the winch's cables and hooks, hover between *Antares* and *Mazury*, and disappear into the mother ship's holds, again and again twenty-four hours a day.

Everything on *Antares* is disconcertingly changed. Fishing is finished. We are tied to the *Mazury*, so even the watch hours are different on the bridge. Franek, or Andrzej, or one of the other fishermen is on the wheel when he is not running the winches. My only duties are to see that the meal hold and freezer hold are emptied and the cargo log tallies with the fishing log once off-loading is done. Transshipping is our last big task before port.

Alcohol from *Mazury*'s sea stores, carried across on the looping rope ladder strung between the two ships, is the biggest change on *Antares*. Rectified spirits, beer, and vodka overtake most of the crew, whose raised voices bounce off the bulkheads in their quarters. Andrzej and Franek insist that I learn to drink vodka like a Slav. Look down into the glass for an instant while you expel all your breath, then throw your head back and swallow all at once, now breathe. If you wish to do as Franek does, breathe out again gently, along your arm. If you drank enough vodka in that one swallow, the hairs will rise. Otherwise, take a drink of water, a sip of coffee or tea, a mouthful of bread, a bite of sausage, a mushroom or two. Now look down into your glass again....

Transshipping continues. The party – *bałagan* – continues during every off-duty moment. Andrzej's watch, Franek's bo's'n's whistle, and a dozen fishermen's shirts are flung overboard. Because, just because. The talk turns to money. Every man on the ship gets a percentage of the crew's share from the fish with Captain Wrona at the top of the list and the others ranked below him to receive zlotys, plus some American dollars for every sea day. Both rates have been recently raised because of the Solidarity strike in the Bering Sea last April, but the money has not kept pace with rising prices in Poland while we have been at sea. Life is brutal and full of traps. Look down into your glass, throw your head back and swallow.

At last the vodka is gone and the holds are empty. *Antares* is loosed from *Mazury* to jog offshore, waiting for orders from Gdynia about proceeding to port. All of us move about the ship drugged by more sleep than we have had in months. Painting, scrubbing, and gear repairs happen in slow motion. My pen crawls across page after page of the trip report: summaries of conversion factor testing; compliance to regulations; modifications to trawl gear; number and type of biological samples; total production of hake on joint venture, supplementary and national fishing; technical descriptions of processing machines and packaging.

The crew and I wander along the decks, gaze at the water, wish urgently now to walk farther and faster or to run. But we are as aware of our limits as the goldfish drifting in aquariums and bowls in almost every cabin on the ship. We have set aside our visions of Vancouver harbour so as not to go mad with impatience, refusing every hint of a world beyond the deck rail. But when the rhythm of *Antares*'s engines alters, increases speed, I lift my head from my pillow immediately to hear the flow of the sea quicken beneath my porthole, then sleep more lightly afterwards.

At dawn on the bridge, the green-smelling air from land blows through both doors and the window over the bow. Race Rocks light shows on our port side. At Constance Bank, the pilot boards and our belief in the possibility of ourselves on shore strengthens, because the pilot's hand-held radio connects him to the Victoria pilot station and to Vancouver Traffic, and because he is a stranger from land, yet he is here with us.

Captain Wrona still bears all the responsibility should anything go wrong with the ship, so he stands behind his helmsman through the long last night of the voyage, watching the course. The captain confirms each of the pilot's orders in English – "amidships," "full ahead," "astern," and "stop engines" are common to all waters – and repeats them in Polish to be certain they are understood by the helmsman. Late in the afternoon, *Antares* passes under Lions Gate Bridge. Vancouver. Captain Wrona breathes the city's name like a sigh. For an instant, his face looks softer, then he turns his attention to the tug at our bow and to Franek and his crew, standing ready to heave the tie-up lines onto Cassiar pier in North Vancouver.

Once the customs officer and the ship's agent have come and gone, everyone but me is in a hurry, besieging the chief steward for dollars, dressing in wrinkled, city clothes to go up to the bar, writing out shopping lists. The Royal Bank's foreign-exchange pamphlet is lying on Captain Wrona's desk when I shake his hand.

I am the only one still moving slowly, folding shirts stiff from the drying line strung over my sink, cramming jeans into duffel bags. The canvas on the bags is worn through here and there from too much travelling in lifeboats, skiffs, and rubber zodiacs, too many hoists up rusted hulls. While Andrzej is beside me, patching the biggest holes with electrician's tape, I still feel part of *Antares*. He helps me carry my gear down the gangplank and we both stagger slightly on the dock. *Gemini*, lying on the other side of the pier, has a telephone for me to call a taxi, which comes before I have time to hesitate or look back.

The green mass of alders along the shore road sustains me against the roar of the cars on the Second Narrows Bridge. The taxi driver doesn't speak, for which I am grateful as the city rushes past the car window.

The house is dusty and silent. I sleep at once, waking before dawn to wonder why our engines have stopped, and return to Cassiar pier later in the morning to say goodbye, as I promised, knowing that *Antares* has no further use for me, knowing Captain Wrona,

Krys, Andrzej, and all of the others are impatient now to leave the ship and Canada and me behind them. The moment I stand again on *Antares*'s curiously still deck and see how innocent the scoured planks appear in the shining city, I believe that I am the only one on the ship who does not know how to exchange one manner of life for another without a backward glance.

While I am buying groceries and choosing library books, the Poles are climbing onto the buses that take them to Vancouver airport, anxious about their seamen's passports and the apricots or kiwi fruit in their bags until they are through Customs. On the LOT jet, they comfort themselves through the long flight thinking of the lighted windows waiting for them in Toruń and Gdynia and other towns.

Antares steams twelve days north to the Bering Sea with her winter captain and crew while in Vancouver, I wake at night whenever the wind changes, dreaming that I am back on the ship, that we are having boat drill, or perhaps we must truly abandon ship and I can't find my life jacket or my boat station. In the pockets of my jeans, months after the voyage, I find squares of soft paper, flattened by the laundry, words still legible: Tow #107 22 metric tons hake; 600 kilograms dogfish? 400 kilograms yellowtail. Coffee beans, grind. Today. Check Loran. Test Line #4. Rybitwa means sea bird.

All winter, the offshore waters move ceaselessly on the edge of my thoughts, secret comfort in the quick, bright city.

ABOUT THE AUTHOR

Joan Skogan has been working at sea since 1987. Her poetry, short fiction and memoirs have appeared in Canadian publications such as *Grain*, *West Coast Review* and *Saturday Night*, and she has been heard speaking about her experiences at sea on CBC Radio. She is the author of *Skeena, A River Remembered*, and the children's books *The Princess and the Sea-Bear* and *Grey Cat at Sea*. She lives in Vancouver.